Contents

*Note: The words which appear in **bold type** in
the text are defined in the Glossary on page 63.*

—1—
Ireland Today: What is Happening?

Most people are vaguely aware of 'The Troubles' in Northern Ireland. Most people have heard of the IRA and the Reverend Ian Paisley. Most people are all too familiar with images of violence and terror from Ireland. Most people are aware that British soldiers patrol the streets of Northern Ireland, where over 400 of them have died since 1971. Most people have the idea that the trouble is 'something to do with religion', with Catholics fighting Protestants.

But very few people are aware of how long ago 'The Irish Problem' started, how far back in history we need to go to find the beginning of the Irish Question. How many of you *really* know what is happening in Northern Ireland? How many of you know why the conflict began? On which side, for example, is the IRA? What religion is Ian Paisley? Where exactly is Northern Ireland?

Who's who in Northern Ireland

Much of our news from Northern Ireland uses various sets of initials, and a good place to start is by looking at these as codes, for the names used by people in Northern Ireland can tell us a great deal.

Any group in Northern Ireland using the word *Ulster* – like the Ulster Volunteer Force (UVF) – will believe that Northern Ireland means the six counties of Ulster and should remain part of Britain. They will regard themselves as British and will almost certainly be Protestant in religion. So will any group using the word *Unionist* – such as the Ulster Unionist Party – for this means they want to continue to see Ulster united with Britain. Generally, such people will describe themselves as Unionists or as *Loyalists* ('loyal' to Britain).

On the other hand, any group using the word *Irish* – like the Irish Republican Army (IRA) – will believe that Northern Ireland should be part of the Republic of Ireland (Eire), not Britain. The same will apply to anyone using the words *Republican* or *Nationalist*. Any group with a Gaelic name – *Sinn Fein*, for instance – will have the same views. Republicans or Nationalists will regard themselves as Irish and will probably be Roman Catholic in religion.

Many other 'labels' also serve as codes in Northern Ireland, even simple everyday things like names, addresses and schools. There are **Gaelic**, Catholic names, such as Sean or Bernadette, and British, Protestant names, such as David or Elizabeth. In large towns like Belfast and Londonderry most Catholics and Protestants live in their own areas. Anyone living in the Falls Road in Belfast, for example, will probably be a Catholic; the Shankill Road almost certainly means a Protestant address. A Protestant will live in Londonderry; a Catholic will call the same city Derry. Most schools are also **denominational** – for one religion. So knowing which school somebody attends can also tell you their religion.

Links: Twentieth Century World History Books
Series Editor: Robert Wolfson

Ireland in Conflict

GCSE Edition

Michael Denning

Hodder & Stoughton

LONDON SYDNEY AUCKLAND TORONTO

Acknowledgements

The Publishers would like to thank the following for permission to reproduce material in this volume:
Andre Deutsch Ltd for the extract from *The Price of My Soul* by Bernadette Devlin; Faber and Faber Ltd for the extract from *Pax Britannica* by James Morris (1968) and the poem 'Whatever You Say, Say Nothing' by Seamus Heaney; K · Griffith for the extract from *Curious Journey* by Griffith and O'Grady (1982); Guardian News Service Ltd for the extracts from *The Guardian*, 14 August 1989, 22 September 1987, 8 July 1987 and 21 November 1985; Hamish Hamilton Ltd for the extract from *Sixty-Eight: The Year of the Barricades* by D Caute (1988); William Heinemann Ltd for the extracts from *The Provisional IRA* by P Bishop and E Mallie; David Higham Associates Ltd for the extracts from *Ireland: A History* by Robert Kee (1980); HMSO for the extracts from 'Disturbances in Northern Ireland' – Report of the Cameron Commission, 1969 and the 'Report of the Widgery Tribunal', 1972; The Irish Times Ltd for the extract from an interview with Lord Brookeborough from the *Irish Times*, 30 October 1968; Drake Marketing Services/Pluto Press for the extract from *Only the Rivers Run Free* by Fairweather, McDonough and McFadyean; Eamon McCann for the extracts from his book *War and an Irish Town*; Pall Mall Press for the extract from *The IRA* by Tim Pat Coogan (1971); Penguin Books Ltd for the extracts from *Ulster* by The Sunday Times Insight Team, copyright Times Newspapers Ltd (1972) and Thames Television for the quote by James Callaghan from *The Troubles*.

Every effort has been made to trace and acknowledge ownership of copyright. The publishers will be glad to make suitable arrangements with any copyright holders whom it has not been possible to contact.

The author and publishers thank the following for permission to reproduce copyright illustrations:
Paddy Allen, *The Guardian*, p 50B; Associated Press Ltd, p 45T; British Library, p 56; Camera Press Ltd, pp 46B, 47, 49B, 50; Hulton Picture Company, pp 26, 31T, 34; Library of Congress, p 25; Mail Newspapers, p 45B; MORI/*Daily Express*, p 61; National Library of Ireland, pp 11, 14T, 16T, 27, 29R, 31B, 37; National Museum of Ireland, pp 16B, 24, 32; National Portrait Gallery, pp 12, 21; Jeremy Nichol, p 39; Pacemaker Press, pp 42(both), 58(both), 59; Popperfoto, pp 18, 19, 43, 46T, 49T, 55(all); Press Association Ltd, p 57T; *Punch*, cover, p 7; Ulster Museum, pp 14B, 29L.

The cover illustration shows a cartoon of Lloyd George from *Punch* magazine.

British Library Cataloguing in Publication Data
Denning, Mike
   Ireland in conflict, – GCSE ed. – (Links : twentieth century world history books).
   1. Northern Ireland. Social conditions
   I. Title II. Series
   941.60824

ISBN 0 340 51811 1

First published 1990

© 1990 Michael Denning

42863

Typeset by Taurus Graphics, Abingdon, Oxon.
Printed in Great Britain for the educational publishing division of Hodder and Stoughton Ltd, Mill Road, Dunton Green, Sevenoaks, Kent by M & A Thomson Litho Ltd, East Kilbride, Scotland.

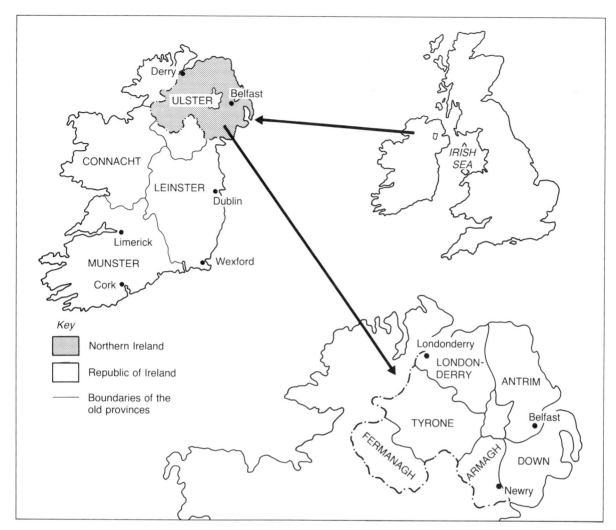

Britain, Ireland and Northern Ireland – the Six Counties

This 'coding' has been summed up very well by the poet Seamus Heaney in a poem called 'Whatever you say, say nothing':

> Smoke-signals are loud-mouthed
>   compared with us
> Manoevrings to find out name and
>   school,
> Subtle discrimination by addresses
> With hardly an exception to the rule
> That Norman, Ken and Sidney
>   signalled Prod
> And Seamus (call me Sean) was sure-
>   fire Pape.
> O land of password, handgrip, wink
>   and nod,
> Of open minds as open as a trap.

EXERCISES

1 Using the information contained in this chapter place the following as Unionists or Nationalists, and explain what their beliefs are likely to be:
  (a) The Irish National Liberation Army
  (b) The Ulster Defence Association
  (c) The Ulster Clubs.
2 Which religion would you expect (a) Ian Paisley (b) Seamus Heaney to be? How did you decide?
3 Can you suggest any reasons why Nationalists dislike the name 'Londonderry'?

—2—
'The Irishman and the Englishman . . .'

'The Irish'

'Have you heard the one about the Irishman . . . ?' How often have you heard 'Irish jokes'? You can buy 'Irish jokebooks' in many ordinary bookshops. Stand-up comedians use the Irish as the subjects of much of their material. Well, it's only a joke, isn't it?

Just think a bit more carefully about some of these jokes. In almost all of them the Irish character is of a particular type. What impression of the Irish is actually given by this humour? Most Irish jokes work on the idea of the 'thick Paddy'. They are only funny because there is an English

stereotype of the Irish.

There is a second English stereotype about the Irish. Look at the cartoon opposite from an English newspaper in 1982. What impression of the Irish does this try to give?

Both of these stereotypes about the Irish have developed over a very long period of time. The cartoon below was published in 1882. Compare it with the one opposite. What similarities do you notice?

'The Irish Frankenstein'

SOURCE 2a

(A Medieval Life of St Bridget, from The Carew Papers, 1575–88, edited by J S Brewer)

When Bridget inquired of her good angel, of what Christian land was most souls damned? The angel showed her a land in the west part of the world . . . For there is no land in the world of so continual war within himself, nor of so great shedding of Christian blood, nor of so great robbing, spoiling, preying, and burning, nor of so great wrongful **extortion** continually, as Ireland.

SOURCE 2b

(Gerald of Wales, History & Topography of Ireland, c.1185)

The Irish are wild, unfriendly people. They live like beasts. They grow little food in their fields. The soil is not to blame but the laziness of the people. Above all people, they cannot be trusted. When they give their word to anyone, they do not keep it. Their beards, clothes and minds are so **barbarous** that they cannot be said to have any culture.

SOURCE 2c

(An Elizabethan writer, c.1581)

The Irish live like beasts . . . are more uncivil, more uncleanly, more barbarous in their customs . . . than in any part of the world that is known.

SOURCE 2d

(Charles Kingsley, 1860)

I am haunted by the human chimpanzees I saw along that hundred miles of horrible country. I don't believe they are our fault. I believe there are not only more of them than of old, but that they are happier, better, more comfortably fed and lodged under our rule than they ever were. But to see white chimpanzees is dreadful; if they were black one would not feel it so much.

SOURCE 2e

(Reginald Maudling, British Home Secretary, 1970)

For God's sake bring me a large Scotch. What a bloody awful country.

Although England and Ireland were neighbours, it is clear that the English and the Irish were very different. Whereas England had been conquered in the early Middle Ages by first the Anglo-Saxons, then the Normans, Ireland had remained largely Gaelic. In England, the old Celtic culture had been displaced, while it survived in Ireland. By the time the

Norman-English arrived in Ireland in the twelfth century, they had little understanding of Ireland's proud Gaelic traditions. And, of course, they came as conquerors. We shall see the importance of this later.

EXERCISES

1 Using the sources in this chapter as evidence, write a short description of the English opinion of the 'typical' Irishman.

2 Do you think Irish jokes do any harm? Explain your answer carefully.

3 Cartoons are not intended to give an accurate picture of an event. How can they still be useful as evidence for historians?

4 Each of the events in the list below may help to explain the attitudes of some of the sources and pictures in this chapter. Copy the chart and match each event with one source to complete it:

Event	Which source does it help explain?	Explanation
1169 Henry II of England attempts to conquer Ireland		
1570 English settlers encouraged to live in Ireland and take land from the Irish		
1859 Publication of Darwin's *Origin of Species*. It seems to suggest that some races are superior to others		
1882 A leading British politician murdered in Dublin		
1969 British troops sent to Northern Ireland		
1982 Eight British soldiers killed by IRA bombs in London		

—3—
A Question of Religion?

What do you think the trouble in Northern Ireland today is actually about?

To many people in Britain the 'Irish Problem' appears to be basically a religious problem, a conflict between Protestants and Catholics. Disputes between religious groups are called **sectarian**. The following extracts from newspaper reports all describe incidents in terms of religion.

It is clear, too, that the Republic of Ireland is a Roman Catholic country, while Northern Ireland is seen, as its first Prime Minister, Sir James Craig, said, as 'a Protestant State'. Religion is obviously involved when Protestant leaders like Ian Paisley protest against visits by the Pope, not only to Northern Ireland, but to Britain and even the European Parliament, calling the Pope 'The scarlet whore of Rome'. Religion is involved when Mrs Hamilton, a follower of Paisley, claims 'the Roman Catholic Church is the anti-Christ', or when Protestants object to a school performance of *The Sound of Music*.

SOURCE 3a

(George McConnell, Democratic Unionist Party, in *The Times*, 1977)

We wish to protest about the staging of *The Sound of Music* in Kilkeel High School. *The Sound of Music* is full of Romanish [Roman Catholic] influences which Protestants hate. At one point candles are lit on stage, some of the children have to appear in the garb of Catholic nuns and they also have to bless themselves publicly in the way the Romans do.

On the other hand, there are differences between Protestants as well. Most Northern Irish Protestants are *Dissenters*, not

Tit-for-tat

The parents of a 22-year-old Roman Catholic shot by Protestant gunmen in north Belfast early yesterday said they believed he was killed in reprisal for the murder of a UDR soldier last week.

James Meighan from the nationalist New Lodge part of west Belfast, was hit twice in the head as he was sitting in his car with his girlfriend close to a UVF stronghold in Ballysillan Road.

The Guardian, *8 July 1987*

Sectarian toll rises in Ulster

The IRA said yesterday that it was responsible for the killing of a Protestant man who, it claimed, was a member of the illegal paramilitary Ulster Volunteer Force and active in sectarian assassinations.

A Protestant woman living in the staunchly Loyalist Lower Shankill area was strung up on a lamp post on Monday night, daubed with paint and beaten with sticks by a Loyalist gang. It is believed that she had a Catholic boy friend.

The Guardian, *22 September 1987*

members of the official Anglican Church of Ireland. Ulster Protestants have also been critical of English Protestants. Many of Paisley's supporters were outraged when Prince Philip played polo on a Sunday.

But is it that simple?

SOURCE 3b

(Lord Brookeborough, former Prime Minister of Northern Ireland, 1968)

Well, there is no discrimination against Roman Catholics [as] Roman Catholics, because they worship in a different way. What there is, is a feeling of resentment ... that most Roman Catholics are anti-British and anti-Northern Ireland. This is nothing to do with religion at all.

SOURCE 3c

(David Caute, *Sixty-Eight: The Year of the Barricades*)

The Yippies [American student leaders] ... met Bernadette Devlin ... Bernadette had explained that the troubles in Ireland had 'nothing' to do with religion.

SOURCE 3d

(Ian Paisley, Protestant leader, 1969)

I want to say that I am anti-Catholic as far as the system of Popery is concerned ... But God being my judge I love the poor **dupes** who are ground down under that system.

SOURCE 3e

(Sean MacStiofain, IRA Chief of Staff, 1972)

People say our campaign is sectarian. I deny that ... as many Catholic members of the RUC have been shot as Protestants. They're shot because they're active agents of British **imperialism** ... The only Protestants we've deliberately killed have been members of the UVF who attacked Roman Catholic areas.

Until the sixteenth century the whole of Europe was Roman Catholic in religion, though there were already differences between England and Ireland. It was a German monk and an English king who helped to change all this.

The Anglican Church

Martin Luther was a monk who refused to accept the authority of the Pope in 1517, and so began what became Protestantism.

A few years later, when King Henry VIII (1509–47) was unable to persuade the Pope to grant him a divorce, he left the Catholic Church, creating instead his own Church of England, the Anglican Church. Henry insisted that his subjects should take an Oath of Supremacy accepting him, not the Pope, as Head of the English Church. For his Catholic subjects, who regarded the Pope as Head of the Church, this was impossible. The King, therefore, came to view Catholics as potential traitors and enemies, especially when England was threatened by other Catholic states – notably Spain. Even today the Queen is Head of the Anglican Church, and the Coronation Oath includes a promise to protect and defend it. Henry VIII was never a Protestant himself, but his son Edward VI and daughter Elizabeth I were. The Irish, however, remained Catholic.

The sixteenth century was an age of religious wars, and from the time of Elizabeth I (1558–1603), Catholics in Britain faced persecution and **discrimination**. Because they could not take the religious oath required by law, Catholics could not become MPs or magistrates. They were not allowed to worship openly as Catholics and were fined if they failed to attend Protestant services. Catholic priests were executed. The government always insisted that they were not punishing people for being Catholics, but for being disloyal. Priests, for example, were not burnt as heretics, but hanged as traitors. Catholics believed that they were suffering as **martyrs** for their faith.

The 'Glorious Revolution'

A change in this position seemed possible in 1685 when a Roman Catholic, James II, became King of England. Catholic relief, however, was short-lived. James was deposed by his son-in-law, the Dutch Protestant William of Orange, in 1688. Using Catholic Ireland as a base, James attempted to regain his throne, but was defeated in 1690 at the Battle of the Boyne. The previous year the Protestant Apprentice Boys of Londonderry had prevented a Catholic army from capturing the city, and James fled into exile in France.

To Protestants it was the 'Glorious Revolution'. To Catholics it was a disaster. William III (1688–1702) passed further laws against Catholics, including 'disabling **papists** from sitting in either House of Parliament'. The Protestant **Ascendancy** had begun.

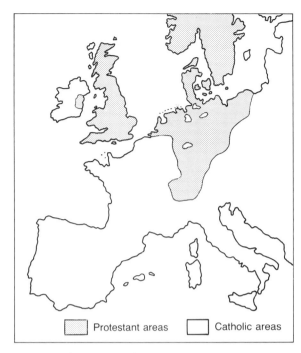

Protestant areas ☐ Catholic areas

Europe in the seventeenth century

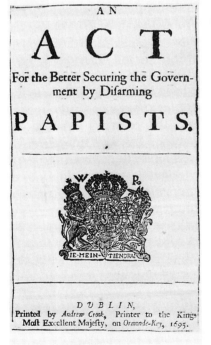

Penal Laws against Catholics

SOURCE 3f

(A ban on Catholics teaching, 1700)

And for a further Remedy against the growth of Popery ... be it further enacted that if any Papist shall take upon themselves the Education of Youth in any place within this Realm being thereof lawfully convicted shall be adjudged to perpetual imprisonment.

The great majority of the Irish still remained Catholic. The laws against them were gradually relaxed. In 1795 some Catholics were given the right to vote – though only for Protestants. Eventually, after a long campaign led by Daniel O'Connell, the British Government accepted Catholic **Emancipation** in 1829, and allowed Catholics to become MPs.

Catholic complaints continued. In Ireland, as in the rest of Britain, the official church was the Anglican Church. This gave it a special position, as it received money from taxes. Catholics objected to paying towards a church to which they did not belong. In fact, so did most Irish Protestants, for few of them were Anglicans either. Most were Presbyterians or Dissenters, who disliked the Church of Ireland just as much as their Catholic neighbours. In 1869 the British Liberal Prime Minister, William Ewart Gladstone, dis-established the Church of Ireland (that is, he took away its special status). The Anglican Church in Ireland was now in the same position as all the other Irish churches. Gladstone was hopeful that this would end religious discontent and go some way towards 'pacifying' Ireland. The next two chapters will consider what else Gladstone saw as being part of the Irish Question.

William Ewart Gladstone

EXERCISES

1 According to sources 3a–3e are the troubles in Northern Ireland only about religion? Explain your answer carefully by referring to the sources.
2 For what reasons did English rulers like Elizabeth I and William III pass laws against Roman Catholics? (Use the map to help you).
3 Write a short conversation between a supporter of Henry VIII and a Roman Catholic with each giving their views about the Oath of Supremacy and their loyalty to the King.

—4—
A Question of Land?

'We will settle the area with legal English and Scottish Protestants who will take an oath to guarantee their loyalty to the King of England'.

These words from King James I in 1607 suggest the second major problem in Ireland – who owned the land. This was important because landowners usually decided how any country was run.

English rulers had worried about invasion from Ireland for centuries, but all attempts to change the Irish, or convert them to the Protestant religion had failed. The Irish remained Gaelic Catholics. England's rulers tried a new approach. If they could not make the Irish English, they would replace them with English settlers. So Protestants from England and Scotland were encouraged to migrate to Ireland, where they were given land taken from the Catholic Irish. This policy of 'plantation' led to a major change in who owned the land in Ireland. The Protestant victory in 1689 confirmed this, and the Penal Laws made it even more difficult for Catholics to own land.

SOURCE 4a

(Penal Laws against Catholics)

No Catholic may bequeath his lands as a whole but must divide it amongst his sons. But if one of these sons becomes Protestant he will inherit the whole estate.

No Catholic can buy land or lease it for more than 31 years.

Look at the pie-charts on this page.

By the nineteenth century, then, most of the land in Ireland was owned by Protestants, many of them living in England. Most Irish Catholics were tenants.

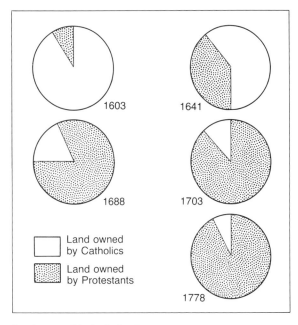

Land ownership in Ireland

They owned no land themselves, but paid rent to landlords for their smallholdings.

Famine

This change came at a time of rapid population growth throughout Europe, and there was a great demand for land. Everywhere, the 1840s came to be known as 'The Hungry Forties': for Ireland, there was the 'Great Hunger', the potato famine of 1845–9. The potato crop was affected by blight in 1845. It then failed almost completely in 1846 and 1847. At least one in ten of the population of Ireland depended on the potato as their staple crop – it was said that in the poorest parts of the west of Ireland it was the only thing the Irish could cook! So the failure of the potato harvest was a terrible disaster for Ireland.

An Irish tenant evicted

Victims of the Famine

SOURCE 4b

(Nicholas Cummins, magistrate, at Skibbereen, County Cork, 1846)

In the first [hut], six famished and ghastly skeletons, to all appearances dead, were huddled in a corner on some filthy straw . . . I approached with horror, and found by a low moaning they were alive – they were in a fever, four children, a woman and what had once been a man . . . in a few minutes I was surrounded by at least 200 such phantoms, such frightful spectres as no words can describe, either from famine or from fever.

SOURCE 4c

(The *Cork Examiner*, 1846)

A countryman, apparently almost deranged, entered a shop . . . and asked for money. Not receiving it he took from under his coat a dead child which he cast upon the counter in desperation, telling her he was unable to procure a coffin for it and immediately fled.

The Act of Union in 1800 had joined Ireland with Britain, which, of course, made the British Government responsible for Ireland, and left them to deal with Famine relief. But while the Irish faced starvation, grain and beef was still being exported from Ireland to England. The British Government refused to give food to the poor; they would only sell it – though much of Ireland had no cash economy. At least 22,000 people died from starvation during the Great Hunger – though the figure was probably far higher – while many more died of diseases related to it.

The failure of the potato crop during the Famine also meant that many Irish tenants were unable to pay their rent to their landlords – who often lived far away in

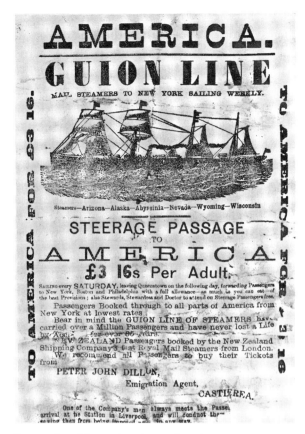

Poster advertising emigration to America

England. A great number of them were evicted from their homes as a result. Many Irish people were driven by poverty to leave Ireland, emigrating to England or America. Nearly four million more emigrated from Ireland in the half century following the Famine.

The Population of England and Ireland		
	Ireland (millions)	England & Wales (millions)
1811	5.9	10
1841	8.2	16
1851	6.5	18
1976	4.7	50

Irish nationalists drew their own conclusions from these events.

SOURCE 4d

(The *Cork Examiner*, 2 November 1846)

Talk of the power of England, her navy, her gold, her resources – oh yes, and her enlightened statesmen, while the broad fact is . . . that she cannot keep the children of her bosom from perishing by hunger. Perhaps indeed Irishmen may not aspire to . . . belonging to the great family of the Empire . . . But when the Queen at her coronation swore to protect and defend her subjects, it is not recollected that . . . there was any exception made with regard to Ireland. How happens it then, while there is a shilling in the Treasury, or even a jewel in the Crown, that patient subjects are allowed to perish with hunger?

SOURCE 4e

(Fintan Lalor, *The Irish Felon*, 1848)

People whose land is in the keeping of others are not safe. The Irish Famine of '46 is proof. The corn crops were sufficient to feed the island. But the landlords would have their rents in spite of the famine and fever. They took the whole harvest and left hunger to their tenants. Had the people of Ireland been the landlords of Ireland, not a single human creature would have died of hunger.

SOURCE 4f

(Robert Whyte, an emigrant to Canada, 1847)

After the grave was filled up, the husband placed two shovels in the form of a cross and said 'By that cross, Mary, I swear to avenge your death. As soon as I earn the price of my passage home I'll go back and shoot the man that murdered you – and that's the landlord'.

SOURCE 4g

(Sir Charles Trevelyan, British official in charge of Famine relief, 1847)

It is my opinion that too much has been done for the people. Under such treatment the people have grown worse instead of better.

Many also felt that the British had deliberately allowed the Famine and emigration to continue, in order to reduce the number of Catholic Irish and so make Ireland easier to govern.

As a result, a Republican called Michael Davitt formed the Land League in 1879. Davitt's League declared a 'Land War' and sought, by protest and violence, to force landlords to set fair rents and stop evictions. It won the support of the leading Irish politician, Charles Stewart Parnell.

SOURCE 4h

(Charles Stewart Parnell, 1879)

A fair rent is a rent the tenant can reasonably afford to pay according to the times, but in bad times a tenant cannot be expected to pay as much as he did in good times.

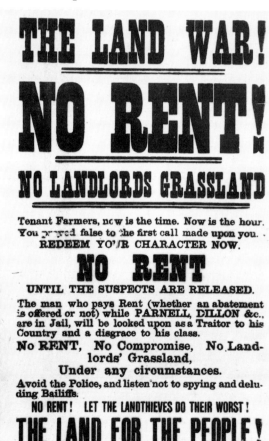

The Land League declares 'War'

Land reform: Mr. Gladstone and the Land League

Eventually, the League hoped to force reforms which would lead to land being given to far more Irish peasants. Rent strikes, **boycotts**, and attacks on landlords forced the Prime Minister, Gladstone, to take notice of the League if he was to '**pacify**' Ireland.

In 1881, a Land Act set up a Commission to fix fair rents and to give loans so that tenants could buy their own land. Between 1881 and 1916, more and more money went towards land reform. By 1916, almost 64 per cent of the population of Ireland owned land. The 'Land Question' seemed to have been answered. But the trouble in Ireland continued.

EXERCISE

1 Design front page reports on the Famine in Ireland in 1849 for two newspapers. One should be an Irish paper (such as the *Cork Examiner*). The other should be an English paper (such as *The Times*). Both should use the evidence in this chapter to consider:

(a) the most important causes of the Famine (include your views on the part played by nature, the landlords, the tenants and the Government)

(b) the consequences of the Famine

(c) any proposals for future action (this should look at the opinions of Trevelyan and Lalor).

—5—
A Question of Government?

'O Paddy dear an' did ye hear the
news that's goin' round?
The **shamrock** is by law forbid to grow
on Irish ground!'

What do these lines from an Irish ballad
suggest about the third part of the Irish
Problem facing Gladstone?

SOURCE 5a

(Oath of the Orange Order, 1795)

I do solemnly and sincerely swear . . . that I will to
the utmost of my powers support and defend the
present King George III and all heirs of the Crown,
so long as they support the Protestant ascendancy,
the constitution and the laws of these Kingdoms.

SOURCE 5b

(The view of Wolfe Tone, 1790)

We are ruled by Englishmen who care only about
the trade of their own country. We have every
resource for trade and manufacture . . . but all in
vain . . . England sacrifices our rights to her lust for
gold and power. If Ireland were free, her trade
and manufactures would spring up like an air
balloon and leave England far behind.

In what ways do the sources above differ
in their attitude towards the connection
between England and Ireland?

The problem of who should govern
Ireland was the third great issue causing
conflict. Should laws for Ireland be made in
Dublin or in London? Was Ireland part of
Britain, or a separate country?

Until Henry VIII's Reformation in the

sixteenth century, English kings had
generally left Ireland under the rule of
Anglo-Irish lords. They controlled the area
known as 'The Pale' – a small area
surrounding Dublin – but most of the rest
of the country remained under the rule of
Gaelic chieftains. The Anglo-Irish tended to
intermarry with the Irish, despite the efforts
of the English king to keep the two groups
apart.

After the Reformation, the rulers of
England took far more interest in Ireland.
Henry VIII declared himself to be King of
Ireland in 1537. English governors were
sent to Dublin, replacing the old Anglo-
Irish barons, and English settlers began to
arrive. New laws tried to 'Anglicise' the
Irish, banning them from speaking Gaelic
or wearing Irish styles of dress.

SOURCE 5c

(Law of Henry VIII, 1537)

And be it enacted that every person shall use the
English tongue and language. And further, be it
enacted that every person having any
house . . . shall keep their houses . . . as near as
ever they can, according to the English order,
condition, and manner.

The victory of William of Orange in 1690
(see Chapter 3) left the Protestants firmly in
control. There was an Irish Parliament, but
since only landowners and Protestants
could vote or become MPs it was run by the
Anglo-Irish. In addition, since 1494 its
powers had been very limited. English laws
automatically applied to Ireland as well,
and the Irish Parliament could only pass

laws agreed by the English Parliament – it could make none of its own.

Ireland had become divided between the 'Orangemen', the Protestant minority which had the political power, and the Catholic Irish majority, which had no say at all in the government of the country. At least one English politician saw this as dangerous.

SOURCE 5d

(The view of Edmund Burke on the division of Ireland 'into two distinct bodies...', 1792)

One was to possess all the franchises [rights], all the property, all the education; the other was to be comprised of drawers of water and cutters of turf for them. Are we to be surprised when by the efforts of so much violence in conquest...we had reduced them to a mob?

The end of the eighteenth century, however, saw two great world events. In 1776 Britain's American colonies rebelled, winning their independence in 1783. The French Revolution followed in 1789, and a series of wars between France and Britain lasted until 1815. The British were worried that similar trouble might start in Ireland and there was, indeed, a rising there. A group called the United Irishmen had formed in 1790 and in 1798 attempted a revolution in Ireland (see Chapter 6).

Five years later, a Protestant organisation, the Orange Order, was set up. Source 5a shows you their oath. They took their name, of course, from William of Orange, 'who saved us from Rogues and Roguery, Slaves and Slavery, Knaves and Knavery, Popes and Popery'. The Orangemen began a tradition of marches, especially in Belfast and Londonderry, to **commemorate** Protestant victories. The 'marching season' in the summer is still a feature of life in Northern Ireland. With their banners and songs, the Orangemen often march through Catholic districts.

A modern wallpainting in Londonderry

An Orange Order march – ~~Londonderry~~, 1969

SOURCE 5e

(A modern Orange Parade song)

If guns were made for shooting,
Then skulls were made to crack.
You've never seen a better Taig [Catholic]
Than with a bullet in his back . . .

What do you imagine the effect of these marches would be on both Protestants taking part and Catholics watching and listening? Orange marches have often led to serious violence in Northern Ireland – in 1849, 1857, 1886, 1920 and 1969, for instance.

In 1800, the Irish Parliament was abolished and an Act of Union made Ireland part of the United Kingdom, with Irish MPs going to the Westminster Parliament, along with English, Scots and Welsh.

Nationalist reaction

From 1800, then, Ireland was seen as part of Britain. This was a situation which many Irishmen did not accept. They believed that Ireland was treated as a colony, and that Irish MPs in a British Parliament were bound to be in a minority. They believed that Ireland could only prosper if it could run its own affairs. This feeling was increased by the confused and muddled way in which the Government tried to deal with the Great Famine of the 1840s. It convinced many of the Irish that Britain neither knew nor cared about Ireland's needs.

Irishmen also hated taxes on Irish linen. These taxes kept the prices high, so that they could not compete with the new textile mills of Lancashire and Yorkshire.

SOURCE 5f

(Fintan Lalor, *The Irish Felon*, 1848)

The landlords do not now and never did belong to this island. **Tyrants** they have been since they first set foot on our soil. I say that the soil of a country belongs to the people of that country.

SOURCE 5g

(James Connolly, a socialist and founder of the Irish Citizen Army, 1915)

Consider what this British Empire is doing. Everywhere it holds down races so that it can prevent them developing their own economies and force them to remain customers of British produce. To do this it stifles India, smothers South Africa and plans the partition of Ireland.

The Protestant landowners of Ireland had been asking for more control over their own affairs for some time, and in 1782 (during the American War of Independence) they had won some concessions. Wolfe Tone, the author of Source 5b, was himself a Protestant. For some of the Protestant ruling class, then, the Act of Union was as unwelcome as it was for many Catholics.

Irish demands for more independence increased after the tragedy of the Famine.

By the time Gladstone decided to 'pacify' Ireland in 1868 he was faced not only with religious grievances and with the demands of the Land League, but also with a growing movement for Home Rule – the right of the Irish themselves to make decisions affecting Ireland. But many of the Protestant Irish feared that Home Rule would take away their privileges and threaten their religion. It was, perhaps, to prove the most difficult problem of them all, and has remained at the heart of the Irish Question.

EXERCISES

1 Copy the following chart and use Chapters 3–5 to match the dates in List A with the events in List B.

List A	List B
1537	Formation of the Orange Order
1607	The Great Hunger
1690	Henry VIII becomes King of Ireland
1795	The Act of Union
1800	The victory of William of Orange
1845	Plantation of Protestant settlers

Beside each, explain the importance of the event.

2 By 1850, Irishmen were divided between Nationalists and Loyalists.
(a) Explain what each would have thought about religious belief, the ownership of land and who should govern Ireland.
(b) What reasons would you give for why the Irish were divided in this way?

3 Would you expect to see the wall painting on page 18 in a Protestant or a Catholic area of Londonderry? Explain why, and explain as fully as you can the symbols on the painting.

4 List the complaints made against British rule by Wolfe Tone in Source 5b. Compare this with Source 5g. What are the similarities?

—6—
Rebellion and Reprisal?

'We fought for justice, and not for
   gain,
But the magistrate sent me away'
   (Irish rock band U2, 'Van Diemen's
                              Land')

Patrick Pearse, the organiser of the Easter
Rising in 1916, claimed that Ireland had

rebelled against British rule six times in 300
years, and would continue to do so until it
won its freedom.

Certainly from the earliest English efforts
to control Ireland to the present day, one
attempted solution to the Irish Question
has always been the use of violence. The
Anglo-Norman knights of the twelfth
century sought to conquer Ireland, and
were involved in a series of battles with the
Gaelic chieftains. This conflict was to
continue off and on until the end of the
sixteenth century.

It was Elizabeth I's attempt to encourage
'plantation' that provoked a major Irish
uprising. The lords of Munster led a revolt
against English settlers in 1581. Many
settlers were killed before the Irish were
defeated, with the English using great
brutality themselves, and 'devastating'
Munster as a punishment. Thousands of
the inhabitants of the province starved as a
result.

SOURCE 6a

(Orders of Sir Henry Sidney in Munster)

. . . the heads of all those which were killed in the
day be cut off from their bodies and brought to
the place where he encamped at night, and should
be laid on the ground by each side of the way
leading to his tent . . . it did bring great terror to
the people when they saw the heads of their dead
fathers, brothers, children, kinsfolk and friends lie
on the ground before their faces.

Queen Elizabeth I

SOURCE 6b

(Edmund Spenser, *The Devastation of Munster*, 1580)

Out of every corner of the woods and glens they came creeping forth upon their hands, for their legs could not bear them; they looked like anatomies [figures] of death . . . they did eat the dead carrions . . . the very carcasses they spare not to scrape out of the graves; and if they found a plot of water-cresses or shamrocks then they flocked as to a feast.

Then in 1595 the last remaining great lord, the powerful Hugh O'Neill, led a great revolt in the north. O'Neill tried to get Spanish help, and won a number of victories over English armies. Eventually, though, he was forced to surrender in 1603, and Ulster became the main area of Protestant settlement. O'Neill himself left Ireland for exile in 1607. The Irish remained unwilling to accept English Protestant rule.

Another serious rising broke out in 1641. For the Irish, this seemed like a good moment, with the likelihood of civil war in England between King Charles I and his Parliament meaning there was little chance of troops from England being sent to help settlers in Ireland. Reports of cruel attacks on the settlers soon reached England. Many of these were exaggerated, but they helped to fuel anti-Catholic feeling.

The Irish also chose to support Charles I during the Civil War which broke out in 1642, as he was more sympathetic to Catholics than his strongly Protestant Puritan opponents. But it was the Puritans who won. Charles was beheaded in 1649 and the new ruler of England, Oliver Cromwell, set out to deal with Ireland. Cromwell gained himself a reputation for cruelty with his ruthless campaign, especially at the capture of Drogheda.

SOURCE 6c

(Oliver Cromwell describing the capture of Drogheda, 1649)

I forbade them to spare any that were in arms in the Town; and, I think, that night they put to the sword about 2000 men; – divers [others] of the officers and soldiers being fled over the Bridge . . . where about 100 of them possessed St. Peter's Church-steeple . . . These being summoned to yield to mercy, refused. Whereupon I ordered the steeple of St. Peter's Church to be fired, when one of them was heard to say in the midst of the flames: 'God damn me, God confound me; I burn, I burn' . . . I am persuaded that this is a righteous judgement of God upon these barbarous wretches.

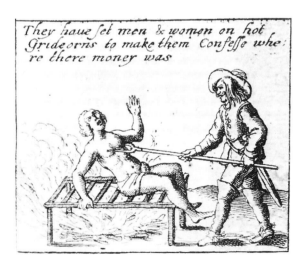

A contemporary print of the Ulster Rising, 1641

Until the eighteenth century the rebellions had been Catholic risings against Protestant settlers. In 1790 a new Irish leader appeared. Wolfe Tone was a Protestant landowner. He was inspired by the revolutions in America and France, both of which stressed the Rights of Man, Liberty and Equality. Tone tried to join Protestant and Catholic together in his 'United Irishmen', aiming to free Ireland from English domination. He sought help from France, and a French army landed in Ireland in 1798. But Tone's rising was badly planned, and too many spies knew about it. He was surprised by the English, and committed suicide to avoid capture.

Using the 'Cat' on a suspected United Irishman

SOURCE 6d

(Wolfe Tone, 1796)

My aim was to break the connection with England, the never failing source of all our political evils, and to assert the independence of my country.

Information about the United Irishmen was obtained in a variety of ways, some of them very brutal.

SOURCE 6e

(From Robert Kee, *Ireland: A History*, 1980)

There was no ceremony used in choosing victims, the first to hand done well enough . . . They were stripped naked, tied to a triangle and their flesh cut through without mercy. And though some stood the torture to the last gasp sooner than become informers, others did not and one single informer in the town was enough to destroy all the United Irishmen in it.

When the 1798 rising was defeated at Vinegar Hill, some 50,000 United Irishmen died – at least half, according to a Protestant clergyman, killed in cold blood.

A second revolt by the United Irishmen took place in 1803. Again, the leader was a Protestant, Robert Emmet. Again, the rising was badly planned and failed. Again, the English punished severely: Emmet himself was hanged, drawn and quartered in Dublin.

Thousands of surviving United Irishmen were transported in prison ships to the newly discovered colony of Australia. According to the Australian historian Robert Hughes, it became 'the official Siberia for Irish **dissidents**'. They endured terrible hardships both on the voyage and in Australia itself.

Before the end of the nineteenth century there had been two more Irish rebellions. In 1848, the European 'Year of Revolutions' and the middle of the Great Famine (see page 13), a group called 'Young Ireland' under William Smith O'Brien (another Protestant) rose in revolt. Like the United Irishmen, they were poorly organised and failed.

The Fenians

More serious was the emergence of a new group of Nationalists after the Famine. The bitterness of Irish exiles led to the formation in America in 1853 of the 'Irish Republican Brotherhood'. In Gaelic, they were known as the 'Fenians', after legendary Gaelic heroes, the Fianna. The oath of the

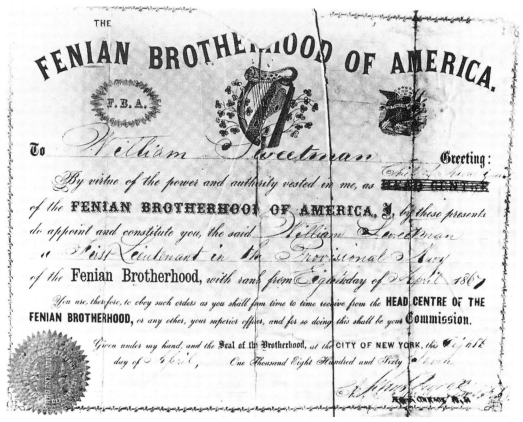

Certificate of membership of the Fenians

Brotherhood made their aims clear: ' . . . in the presence of God, to renounce all allegiance to the Queen of England, and to take arms and fight to make Ireland an Independent Democratic Republic'.

The Fenians grew in strength in America and Ireland. Several of their leaders fought in the American Civil War of 1861–5, and gained military experience. By 1867 their leader, James Stephens, believed that they were ready, and a rebellion was planned.

The Fenian Rising in Ireland failed, but it won great publicity in mainland Britain. A bomb planted outside Clerkenwell gaol in London to free Fenian prisoners killed 30 people. In Manchester a policeman was killed when a band of Fenians successfully rescued two of their arrested leaders. Although it was never proved who fired the shot, three Irishmen were tried and executed for murder. To the British, these were the 'Fenian Outrages'; to the Irish, the executed men became the 'Manchester Martyrs', and joined Tone and Emmet as Nationalist heroes.

Were the Fenians the first Irish 'terrorists'? Or were they Irish patriots?

SOURCE 6f

(Charles Stewart Parnell, 1877)

I do not believe, and never shall believe, that any murder was committed at Manchester.

Long before the emergence of the IRA and the start of 'The Troubles' then, Ireland had a long tradition of violence between Nationalists seeking independence and the British. Every Irish rebellion increased British fear, and every British reprisal increased Irish hatred: a vicious circle had been created. But by the time of the Fenian Rising other Irish Nationalists were searching for other solutions.

IRELANDS LATEST MARTYRS.
EXECUTED AT MANCHESTER ENG? NOV. 23RD 1867 THEIR LAST PRAYER
"GOD SAVE IRELAND."

The Manchester Martyrs remembered

EXERCISES

1 Copy and complete the following chart to sort out the main information from this chapter.

Date	Who rebelled and why?	Results of rebellion

2 Do you think that religion was the main reason for the rebellions between the sixteenth and nineteenth centuries? Explain your answer.

3 'The moment the very name of Ireland is mentioned, the English seem . . . to act with the barbarity [cruelty] of tyrants and the fatuity [stupidity] of idiots'.
(a) Using extracts from the sources in this chapter, what evidence can you find to support the idea that the English treated Ireland cruelly or foolishly?
(b) Why do you suppose English leaders used the methods they did?

4 The Fenian Rising of 1867 failed. Why, then, is it an important event in Irish history?

—7—
Home Rule?

Neither the failure of the Fenians nor the reforms carried out by Gladstone (see pages 12 and 16) ended discontent in Ireland. Irish Nationalists continued to see Ireland as a colony ruled by Britain with little regard for the native inhabitants.

SOURCE 7a

(From James Morris, *Pax Britannica*, 1968)

The population of Ireland had been 8 million in 1841: it was 5 million in 1897. Its literacy rate was little higher than Burma's. Its death rate was actually rising, and Dublin's was higher than any other European city's . . . its countryside, one of the most fertile in Europe, was neglected and dilapidated – more than 60 per cent of it given up to grass, a proportion unparalled in the world, and only about 11 per cent ploughed. The chief ambition of young Irishmen was simply to leave . . . Marriages were fewer, and happened later, than in any other country: of women between 15 and 45 only one in three was married.

But the Fenian Rising did seem to prove that there was little point in rebellion. Instead, a new Irish leader decided on a new tactic.

Charles Stewart Parnell, like Tone and Emmet before him, was a Protestant. He was MP for County Meath, and a leader of the Home Government Association, later the Home Rule Party. Parnell decided that if the British would never agree to Irish independence, they might be persuaded to accept Home Rule. This meant that Ireland would remain part of the United Kingdom, and that Britain would still make the major decisions, for instance on foreign affairs. But on matters that concerned Ireland, the Irish would be able to decide their own policies.

SOURCE 7b

(Aims of the Home Government Association, 1873)

It is essentially necessary to the peace and prosperity of Ireland that the right of domestic legislation on all Irish affairs should be restored to our country.

Even if Home Rule was less than Irish Nationalists like the Fenians wanted, it could be seen as a stepping-stone towards independence.

Charles Stewart Parnell

SOURCE 7c

(Parnell on Home Rule, 1885)

No man has the right to fix the boundary to the march of a nation. No man has the right to say to this country: 'Thus far shalt thou go and no further'. When we have undermined English misgovernment, we have paved the way for Ireland to take her place among the nations of the earth. And let us not forget that it is the ultimate goal at which all we Irishmen aim . . . None of us . . . will be satisfied until we have destroyed the last link which keeps Ireland bound to England.

It had been clear since the Act of Union (see page 19) that 100 Irish MPs could always be outvoted in Parliament at Westminster. But it was also clear to Parnell that if they were sufficiently well organised they could make life very difficult for any government. Parnell's Irish Party used simple tactics – but they used them very effectively. They decided that if Parliament refused to discuss Home Rule, then the Irish MPs would make sure that nothing else could be discussed either! Parnell and his followers began the 'filibuster', taking turns to make endless speeches in the House of Commons about all sorts of topics. This meant that all the time allowed for debate was used up, and no votes could be taken. Thanks to the Irish MPs, the debate on the Queen's Speech in 1880 lasted for eleven nights! Normal parliamentary business became impossible.

Outside Parliament, Parnell was also President of the Land League (see page 16). Under pressure from both groups, the Prime Minister, Gladstone, clearly had a problem. At first he turned to force (coercion). Parnell himself was imprisoned in 1881. But eventually Gladstone was convinced that Home Rule might indeed be a way to 'pacify Ireland'. Parnell was released, the Irish Party supported Gladstone, and in 1886 a Home Rule Bill was brought before Parliament.

Home Rule faced fierce opposition, however. In Ireland itself most Protestants feared that Home Rule would lead to a Catholic controlled Irish parliament. They believed that 'Home Rule means Rome Rule' and that their whole way of life would be threatened. The Orange Order grew in strength and a new party was set up to fight Home Rule in 1885. This was the Irish Unionist Party, led by Sir Edward Carson.

SOURCE 7d

(A statement by Belfast industrialists, 1893)

As part of the UK we have shared in the progress of industry in the great centres of England. How would our commercial interests be represented in a parliament in Dublin? We all know Ireland is an agricultural country. We are not prepared to come under the rule of a Dublin parliament dominated by poor farmers.

Carson's Unionists could count on the support in Britain of the Conservative Party. The Conservatives feared that Home Rule would be a first step in the break-up of the British Empire by encouraging other colonies like India to make similar demands. One of their leaders, Lord Randolph Churchill, promised Carson the support of the Conservatives, stating in 1886 that 'Ulster will not be a consenting party . . . Ulster will fight, Ulster will be right'.

Many members of Gladstone's own Liberal Party also opposed Home Rule. The issue split the party, with Joseph Chamberlain and others leaving the

Lord Randolph Churchill and opposition to Home Rule

Liberals to join the Conservatives. The Bill of 1886 was defeated in the House of Commons.

Gladstone tried once more in 1893. This time the Home Rule Bill passed the House of Commons, but was defeated in the House of Lords, most of whose members were Conservatives. It was the end of Gladstone's long career, and the Conservatives won the election of 1894. Parnell's career was ended, too, by a divorce scandal. With the Conservatives in power, it looked as if the battle for Home Rule was lost.

For the next decade the Conservatives tried to 'kill Home Rule by kindness'. More land reforms helped Irish tenants to buy their own land. Ireland grew more prosperous. Even when the Liberals regained power in 1906 there was little prospect of Home Rule. The Liberal majority was so big that they did not need the support of the Irish Party, now led by John Redmond.

But all of this was changed by the election of 1910.

1910 Election Results	
Conservative Party	272
Liberal Party	272
Irish Party	84
Labour Party	42
Unionist Party	22

These results meant that no one party could form a government without the support of some of the others. The Conservatives could count on the support of the Unionists; the Liberals would probably be able to get the backing of Labour. But the balance of power was held by the Irish Nationalists. Without them, neither the Conservatives nor the Liberals could govern. And the price of their support, of course, was another attempt at Home Rule.

The Third Home Rule Bill

At this time, the Liberals were involved in a battle with the Conservative House of Lords, which had refused to pass the 1909 Budget. Eventually, in 1911, a new law reduced the power of the Lords. They could no longer reject Bills altogether; at most they could now delay a law for two years. This meant that if another Home Rule Bill passed the House of Commons, it would become law whatever the House of Lords did. The fate of the second Home Rule Bill could not be repeated. A third Home Rule Bill was introduced by the Liberals in 1912. It was passed by the Commons, then rejected by the Lords – but would therefore become law in September 1914. The battle for Home Rule seemed to be won.

In Ireland the Unionists had no intention of accepting this outcome. The majority of Irish Protestants lived in Ulster, and it was there that Carson found his strongest support. In 1912, the Unionists drew up their Solemn League and Covenant, pledging themselves to resist Home Rule. Carson announced that when Home Rule became law, the Unionists would set up their own government in Ulster.

SOURCE 7e

(The Solemn League and Covenant, 1912)

Being convinced that Home Rule would be disastrous to the material well-being of Ulster, as well as the whole of Ireland, subversive [destructive] of our political and religious freedom ... We men of Ulster pledge to stand by one another in defending our position in the United Kingdom.

SOURCE 7f

(Carson resists Home Rule, September 1911)

We must be prepared ... the morning Home Rule passes, ourselves to become responsible for the government of the Protestant province of Ulster.

To back up these claims, the Unionists

Carson signs the Covenant

Oglaigh na hEireann.

ENROL UNDER THE GREEN FLAG.

Safeguard your rights and liberties (the few left you).

Secure more.

Help your Country to a place among the nations.

Give her a National Army to keep her there.

Get a gun and do your part.

JOIN THE

IRISH VOLUNTEERS

(President: EOIN MAC NEILL).

The local Company drills at

Ireland shall no longer remain disarmed and impotent.

Recruiting for the Irish Volunteers

created a private army, the Ulster Volunteer Force. In the rest of Ireland, the Nationalists replied with their own force, the Irish Volunteers. The old Irish Republican Brotherhood was also revived.

In 1913, both sides equipped themselves with illegal shipments of weapons. Ireland seemed to be nearing civil war. If the Home Rule Bill did become law, it seemed the Unionists were prepared to fight to resist it; if it did not, then the Nationalists would fight to force the Government to keep its promise. The position was made even more difficult for the Government as it did not wish to use force itself against people whose aim was to remain British, and who insisted on their loyalty to Britain! In any case, many officers in the British Army sympathised with the Unionists, and it was far from certain that they would be prepared to use force against them. The 'Curragh Mutiny' of 1914 saw a number of officers threaten to resign rather than fight the Unionists.

Then, in August 1914, one month before Home Rule was due to become law, Britain declared war on Germany and the First World War began.

EXERCISES

1 Is there any evidence in the sources that Parnell wanted more than Home Rule for Ireland?

2 Draw up a list of arguments for and against Home Rule from both the Irish and British points of view.

3 Does the cartoon on page 27 support or oppose the actions of Lord Randolph Churchill? Explain how you can tell.

4 The Home Rule Bill should have become law in September 1914. What should the Government have done? Consider the options below, then for each write a summary of their likely results, if put into practice. Then say which course of action you would have recommended to the Government.

Options	Likely results
(a) Allow Home Rule to become law	
(b) Forget about Home Rule altogether	
(c) Postpone Home Rule until the end of the war. (Remember, you do not expect the war to last very long!)	

—8—
Independence?

Many Unionists and Nationalists agreed to forget the battle over Home Rule until the end of the European war, and volunteered to fight in the British Army. However, one group of Nationalists took a different decision. They believed that the postponement of Home Rule was another British trick, and proof that Britain would never keep its promises. These Nationalists became even more suspicious when the Unionist leader, Carson, was given a place in the British Cabinet.

SOURCE 8a

(James Connolly, Irish Citizen Army, 1914)

We have no foreign enemy except the treacherous government of England – a government that even whilst it is calling us to die for it, refuses to give a straight answer to our demand for Home Rule.

SOURCE 8b

(Sean Kelly, Irish Volunteers, 1914)

... three weeks after the war had started a meeting was held at which it was decided that Ireland should make use of the opportunity of the European war to rise in **insurrection** against England.

These Republicans followed the ideas of Sinn Fein ('Ourselves Alone') – that Home Rule was not enough. What they wanted was complete independence for Ireland. A number of them also felt that the peaceful tactics of the Home Rule Party had failed to achieve anything. The failure of the British Government and Army to act against the Ulster Volunteer Force had convinced them that Britain really sided with the Unionists,

and had no real intention of allowing even Home Rule.

The leaders of this group of Republican Nationalists looked back to the tradition of physical force, and revived the Irish Republican Brotherhood. Every year they visited the grave of Wolfe Tone.

SOURCE 8c

(Patrick Pearse, a Gaelic poet, at the graveside of Wolfe Tone in 1913)

We have come here not merely to salute ... the noble spirit of Tone. We have come to express once more our full acceptance of the gospel of Irish Nationalism ... we need not re-state our programme; Tone has stated it for us: 'To break the connection with England, the never failing source of all our evils'.

Tone was not the only hero of the Irish Volunteers. The old Fenian O'Donovan Rossa died in 1915, and was given a hero's burial. Seventeen special trains brought mourners and a guard of honour in military uniform fired a salute over the grave. Pearse again made a speech at the graveside.

SOURCE 8d

(Patrick Pearse at the graveside of O'Donovan Rossa in 1915)

Life springs from death and from the graves of patriot men and women spring living nations. The Defenders of the Realm ... think they have pacified Ireland ... but the fools, the fools, the fools, they have left us our Fenian dead and while Ireland holds these graves, Ireland unfree shall never be at peace.

The Easter Rising

Pearse, Connolly and their followers hoped to get weapons and help from Germany, and planned a rising in Dublin for Easter 1916. A British diplomat who was sympathetic to the Irish cause, Sir Roger Casement, persuaded the Germans to help, but the ship bringing him and 20,000 rifles was captured by the British Navy a week before Easter. Casement himself was hanged. The British now knew what was planned, but Pearse and Connolly decided to go ahead with the rebellion. On Easter Monday, the rebels took control of several points in Dublin, including the Post Office. From there, Pearse announced the creation of an Irish Republic: 'We declare the right of the people of Ireland to the ownership of Ireland . . . we hereby proclaim the Irish Republic as a Sovereign Independent State, and we pledge our lives and the lives of our comrades-in-arms to the cause of its freedom'.

The rebels were heavily outnumbered by British troops – within 48 hours the odds against them were 20–1. Even so, there was a week of fierce fighting, during which a great deal of damage was caused to the centre of Dublin. The rebels then surrendered 'to prevent the further slaughter of Dublin citizens, and in the

Dublin GPO after the Easter Rising

hope of saving the lives of our followers now surrounded and hopelessly outnumbered'. 300 civilians, 60 rebels and 130 British soldiers had been killed.

But had the rebels expected to win? Look carefully at the following sources about their motives in 1916.

SOURCE 8e

(Patrick Pearse)

Ireland will not find Christ's peace until she has taken Christ's sword . . . We must not faint at the sight of blood. Winning through it, we (or those of us who survive) shall come unto great joy.

. . . Well, when we are all wiped out, people will blame us for everything, condemn us . . . [but] after a few years, they will see the meaning of what we tried to do.

Patrick Pearse and his brother

Execution of one of the 1916 rebels

SOURCE 8f

(James Connolly)

We are going out to be slaughtered.

Immediately after the Rising, the captured rebels were very unpopular in Dublin. But what were the British going to do with them? The army in fact held a series of secret trials, and sentenced 77 of the rebels to death. Fifteen of them were eventually shot by firing squads, including Pearse and Connolly, who had been so badly wounded that he was unable to stand and had to be strapped to a chair for his execution. Public opinion began to change.

SOURCE 8g

(Tom Barry, later IRA member, *Curious Journey*, 1982)

In 1916 I was in Mesopotamia with the British [Army] . . . I saw a notice. It told us of this rising in Dublin, and the executions of men I'd never heard of – I said to myself, 'What the hell am I doing here with the British Army? It's with the Irish I should be!'

SOURCE 8h

(John Dillon, Home Rule Party MP)

What is happening is that thousands of people in Dublin, who ten days ago were bitterly opposed to the whole of the Sinn Fein movement, and to the rebellion, are now becoming infuriated against the Government on account of the executions.

SOURCE 8i

(W B Yeats, extract from 'Easter 1916')

Was it needless death after all?
For England may keep faith
For all that is done and said.
We know their dream; enough
To know they dreamed and are dead;
And what if excess of love
Bewildered them till they died?
I write it out in verse –
MacDonagh and MacBride
And Connolly and Pearse
Now and in time to be,
Wherever green is worn,
Are changed, changed utterly:
A terrible beauty is born.

TIMECHART	
Events in Ireland	**Events in the First World War**
	April 1915 British defeated at Gallipoli
	Battle of Ypres
May 1915 Irish Republican Brotherhood plans Easter Rising	**February–December 1916** Battle of Verdun
April 21 1916 Arrest of Casement	
April 24 1916 Easter Rising starts	
April 29 1916 Surrender of rebels	Surrender of British Army at Kut (Mesopotamia)
May 3–12 1916 Executions of rebels	**July 1916** Battle of the Somme

SOURCE 8j

(General Election results in Ireland)

The parties	1910	1918
Sinn Fein	3 seats	73 seats
Unionists	22 seats	26 seats
Home Rule Party	80 seats	6 seats

Just as the Orangemen look back to the siege of Londonderry and the Battle of the Boyne, so Irish Republicans look back to the Easter Rising of 1916.

EXERCISES

1 (a) Historical events have many causes. Some of these will be long-term and some short-term. With your teacher's help, divide the following list into long and short-term causes of the Easter Rising, and explain the difference between the two types:

the Act of Union, 1800
the start of the First World War, 1914
the Famine, 1845–9
the postponement of Home Rule, 1914
the arming of the Irish Volunteers and UVF, 1912–13
Irish Nationalism, 1798–1916

(b) Choose any three of these events and explain how they helped to cause the Easter Rising.

2 People who take part in historical events also have their own individual motives or reasons.

(a) Do the sources suggest that Connolly and Pearse expected to defeat the British Army in 1916? If not, why did they still go ahead with the Easter Rising?

(b) Why do you think the British took the decisions they did after the Rising had been put down? Use the date chart to help you.

3 Look at Sources 8g–8j. From the evidence, would you say that Pearse was right, and that attitudes towards Irish Republicanism were changed by the Easter Rising? Explain your answer carefully.

—9—
Ireland Divided?

The election of 1918 showed that Nationalist feeling in Ireland was too strong to be ignored. Sinn Fein's **manifesto** had made its aims quite clear.

SOURCE 9a

(Sinn Fein manifesto)

Sinn Fein aims at securing the establishment of the Irish Republic.

1 By withdrawing the Irish Representatives from the British Parliament, and by denying the right and opposing the will of the British Government . . . to legislate for Ireland.
2 By making use of . . . every means . . . to render impotent [powerless] the power of England to hold Ireland in **subjection** by military force or otherwise.

The Sinn Fein MPs refused to go to Westminster. Instead they set up their own parliament – the *Dail Eireann* – in Dublin, and attempted to take control of the country. In many areas they were extremely successful, setting up their own police force, law courts, and so on.

Equally, though, Unionist support during the war and the strength of their own following in Ulster made them hard to ignore. To make matters even more complicated, Britain was now ruled by a **coalition** government. The old Liberal Party was split, and the Prime Minister, Lloyd George, could survive only with Conservative support. The Conservatives, of course, were determined to support Unionist opposition to Home Rule.

While the Government decided what to do, Irish Nationalists took action. On 21 January 1919, two policemen in County Tipperary were ambushed and shot. Their killers were members of the newly formed Irish Republican Army, and the attack was described by one of them, Dan Breen, as 'the first deliberate planned action by . . . the Irish Volunteers renewing the armed struggle, temporarily suspended, after Easter Week 1916'.

The IRA had arrived. Led by Michael Collins, the IRA attacked British officials, especially the police. By the middle of 1920, some 200 members of the Royal Irish Constabulary were resigning each month. IRA 'Flying Columns' moved swiftly throughout Ireland, fighting a **guerrilla** war.

Michael Collins

Collins intended to make it impossible for the British to govern Ireland.

The British replied by sending a new army to Ireland to combat the IRA. It consisted largely of ex-soldiers called Auxiliaries, but nicknamed the 'Black and Tans' from the colour of their uniform. They soon gained a reputation for brutal behaviour and there were protests about their use even in England. On the morning of 21 November 1920 the IRA 'executed' twelve British secret service officers. In the afternoon the Black and Tans opened fire on a football crowd in Dublin, killing twelve spectators and wounding sixty more. This day was Ireland's first 'Bloody Sunday'. After Tom Barry's 'Flying Column' ambushed and killed sixteen Black and Tans in County Cork, the Auxiliaries retaliated by burning half of the town of Cork.

SOURCE 9b

(Labour Party Commission on Ireland, January 1921)

Things are being done in the name of Britain which must make her name stink in the nostrils of the world.

SOURCE 9c

(Archbishop of Canterbury, February 1921)

The Government's policy is morally unjust. If you get peace by wrong-doing then you have not really won a peace that is worthwhile.

In Ireland, the actions of the Black and Tans only increased support for the IRA. In the elections of May 1921, Sinn Fein won every seat but one outside the six counties of Ulster. Besides, with the end of the Great War the last thing most people in Britain wanted was another war in Ireland, especially when it became clear that there would be no quick victory.

IRA support was increased with the deaths of new Nationalist 'martyrs'. Terence McSwiney, the Sinn Fein mayor of Cork, died on hunger strike in prison. Kevin Barry, a teenage IRA man executed by the British, also became a Republican hero.

Lloyd George was advised that it would take a full-scale war and an army of 100,000 men to reconquer Ireland. His own commander in Ireland suggested that a

Protest at executions of IRA prisoners

military victory over the IRA was almost impossible. Even if the IRA was defeated, could the massive support for Sinn Fein be ignored? If it was, how long would it be before Ireland exploded again?

Partition

Lloyd George chose instead to try a new answer. He decided to divide Ireland in two – to *partition* it, keeping Ulster united with Britain, but creating a new Free State in the rest of Ireland.

Neither the Unionists nor the Nationalists really wished to see Ireland divided. But there were good reasons for both to be tempted by this offer. The Unionists were soon convinced that to refuse might mean Ulster becoming part of a Catholic-Nationalist Ireland. They were, after all, heavily outnumbered in Ireland as a whole, but formed a majority in much of Ulster.

If you look at the cartoon of Lloyd George on the front cover and map on the next page, you will notice that the Ulster accepted by the Unionists was in fact different from that first proposed by Lloyd George. Try to work out why.

Even if the Unionists did not much like Partition, however, they soon came to see it as the only way of keeping their 'British' identity.

SOURCE 9d

(The population of Ulster by religion in 1921)

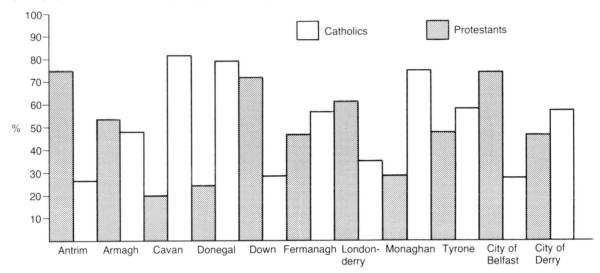

SOURCE 9e

(The Democratic Unionist Party, *Irish Unification – Never*, 1984)

The idea that Ireland must be ruled as one unit is totally false. Northern Ireland is utterly different from the Republic of Ireland . . . It dates from 'The Ulster Plantation' in the early years of the seventeenth century. These settlers brought with them a way of life which was totally different to that in the rest of Ireland.

For the Nationalists, the choice was harder. They regarded Ulster as one of the provinces of Ireland, and for many of them Ireland could never be complete without it. On the other hand, this was a chance to get most of the country. If they refused and carried on the war, could the IRA be sure of victory? Would Ulster, in time, be added to the rest of an Irish state? Was this the best deal they were likely to get? The war had been costly for both sides: 600 men on the British side had been killed, with over 1,000 wounded; the IRA had lost 752 dead and 866 wounded.

Collins and most of the IRA leaders decided to accept the Partition Treaty in 1921, with Collins becoming the first President of the Irish Free State. What they gained was basically Home Rule. They accepted the British King, but were able to make their own laws for the 26 counties of the Free State. They had to accept an Ireland without Ulster, though they would not accept that this had to be permanent. They were also confident that the Boundary Commission which was to be set up would transfer the largely Nationalist counties of Fermanagh and Tyrone to the new state.

Ulster before and after Partition

— 36 —

But a minority of Republicans, led by De Valera and Liam Lynch, rejected the Treaty.

SOURCE 9f

(The Republican leader Michael Collins accepts the Treaty, January 1922)

Think – what have I got for Ireland? Something which she has wanted these past 700 years. Will anyone be satisfied at the bargain? Will anyone? I tell you this – early this morning I signed my own death warrant.

SOURCE 9g

(Sean MacEntee, Republican, speech to the Dail, 1921)

Mark my words, under this Treaty Ulster will become England's fortress in Ireland . . . I have heard much of our gradual growth to freedom under this, how we will **encroach** a little here and crawl a little there until we attain the full measure of our liberties. I tell you that so long as Ulster [exists separately] . . . you will not budge one inch . . .

When the Partition Treaty came into force, a new civil war broke out, this time in the Free State between the rival groups of the IRA. The fighting was just as fierce as it had been against the British. Michael Collins himself was ambushed and killed in 1922. He had indeed signed his own death warrant. Liam Lynch also died in the fighting, and the Nationalist government found itself executing Irish Republicans, just as the British had done. It was only after two years of warfare that peace came to the new Irish Free State with the defeat of the Anti-Treaty Republicans.

Fifteen years later, in 1937, the Free State declared itself to be an independent Republic of Eire. De Valera had become Prime Minister in 1932, after being sentenced to death by the British in 1916 and imprisoned by the Free State from 1923–4. It was under his leadership that the IRA was banned in 1936. During the Second World War (1939–45) Eire stayed neutral, and its final links with Britain ended in

DAN BREEN'S APPEAL

D. BREEN'S APPEAL TO HIS OLD COMRADES NOW IN THE FREE STATE ARMY.

Comrades,
ARE YOU AWARE that you are fighting against the Republic that you fought to establish in 1916, and that was maintained and is going to be maintained?
ARE YOU AWARE that England tried to disestablish the Republic through a reign of Black and Tan terror?
ARE YOU AWARE that she is now using the so-called Provisional Government to try where she failed?
ARE YOU AWARE that YOU are the Black and Tans of to-day, the only difference is the uniform?
ARE YOU AWARE that the death of CATHAL BRUGHA is a damnable and eternal stain on the uniform?
ARE YOU AWARE that CATHAL BRUGHA died as my comrade, SEAN TREACY, died?-- no surrender to enemies of the Republic was their cry.
ARE YOU AWARE that there are hundreds of MEN who will die as Brugha and Treacy died in defence of the Republic?
ARE YOU AWARE that I did my best to maintain the army for the Republic, but I failed because your section took orders from our only enemy--England?
Comrades, I thought my term of soldiering was over, but duty again called me to defend the Republic, which I will do or die in the attempt.
Will you again stand with me as my comrades in arms, or will you continue to fight with England against me?

An anti-Treaty Republican poster, 1922

1948, when the Republic of Ireland was accepted by the British as a sovereign state. At last the Nationalist dream of Wolfe Tone and Robert Emmet, of James Stephens and Charles Stewart Parnell, of Patrick Pearse and James Connolly, had been realised. Except, of course, for the question of Ulster.

EXERCISES

1 List as many reasons as possible for Lloyd George's decision to divide Ireland. Now place these in order of importance and write a paragraph to explain your order.
2 (a) Explain the main points for and against the Partition Treaty for Sinn Fein. Sources 9f and 9g will help.
   (b) Explain why the Unionists were prepared to accept a smaller Ulster. Sources 9d and 9e will help.
3 Was the Treaty of 1922 a victory for the Republicans, for the Unionists or for the British? Explain your answer carefully.
4 How successful was Partition as an answer to the Irish Question? (Think carefully about events in Ireland today.)

—10—

The Orange State

SOURCE 10a

(Lord Craigavon, first Prime Minister of Northern Ireland, 1934)

I have always said I am an Orangeman first and a politician and member of this parliament afterwards . . . all I boast is that we are a Protestant parliament and a Protestant state.

SOURCE 10b

(Sir George Clark, Grand Master of the Orange Order)

I would draw your attention to the words 'civil and religious liberty'. This liberty as we know it is the liberty of the Protestant religion.

The Unionist leader, Sir James Craig (later Lord Craigavon), became the first Prime Minister of Ulster which had its own Parliament, at Stormont in Belfast, after Partition. However, although Ulster was a Unionist state, it included a large Catholic minority – about a third of the population. This minority also had a higher birth rate than the Protestant majority. Most Catholics were Nationalists who disagreed with an Ulster divided from the rest of Ireland. Ulster was small and economically weak, and many people doubted if it could survive for long without the rest of Ireland. The Free State itself still saw Ireland as one country, and insisted that, sooner or later, Ulster would be reunited with it.

How would the new Protestant state treat those in Ulster who disagreed with a divided Ireland? How would the Unionist leaders make sure that Ulster remained a Protestant state?

Partition was followed in Ulster, as in the rest of Ireland, by a wave of violence. There had always been trouble between Protestants and Catholics in Belfast, and on 12 July 1920 a Protestant gang attacked Catholic workers at a Belfast shipyard. Between that date and July 1922, 453 people were killed in Belfast alone – 257 Catholics, 157 Protestants, 37 policemen or soldiers, and two unknown. A familiar pattern was established as Catholics turned for protection to the IRA, the only body that seemed willing or able to resist the Protestant mobs. In 1935, 15 years after Partition, rioting in Belfast remained so serious that British troops had to be sent to help restore order.

The Unionists blamed the Nationalists for the violence, and used it as an excuse to introduce tough security measures. Craig persuaded the British to set up a special, armed part-time police force to help the Royal Ulster Constabulary. The 'B-Specials' were made up of 'well-disposed citizens', which inevitably meant Loyalists. Often, these were former members of the UVF, and were soon as feared and distrusted by Catholics as the Black and Tans had been. The RUC itself was also almost entirely Protestant – only one policeman in six was a Catholic. Almost all judges were Unionists. Even in 1970, three out of seven Ulster judges were former Unionist MPs; a fourth

Wall painting in Londonderry, 1989

was the son of a Unionist minister. Finally, the British Government passed the Special Powers Act of 1922. It said:

1 People suspected of crime could be arrested and kept in prison without a trial for as long as the Government wished. (This was known as **internment**).
2 Newspapers could be prevented from printing certain reports.
3 Houses could be searched without a warrant.
4 The authorities did not have to hold inquests on any dead bodies found in Northern Ireland.

How could each of these measures have been used against Nationalists in Northern Ireland? The 'Orange State' had been established.

To many of the Unionists who had followed Carson in resistance to Home Rule, all Catholics were suspected of being supporters of Sinn Fein. As a result, it was felt that they could not be loyal to British

Ulster. The only way, therefore, of keeping Ulster out of a Nationalist Ireland was to keep it Protestant.

But if Ulster was to be a Protestant state, the Unionists had to keep political control. To begin with, local elections in Northern Ireland used **proportional representation** as a way of protecting the minority. In 1920, Nationalists were voted into power in 25 out of 80 councils in Ulster. Craig responded by abolishing proportional representation in 1922, and redrawing the boundaries for elections. These 'gerrymandered' boundaries made it very difficult for Catholics to win.

Look carefully at the map showing Londonderry wards on the next page.

What results might be expected in elections for Londonderry Council? How would these results compare with the population of Londonderry?

The Cameron Report, written by a British judge in 1969, strongly condemned this gerrymandering, describing it as the 'deliberate manipulation of local

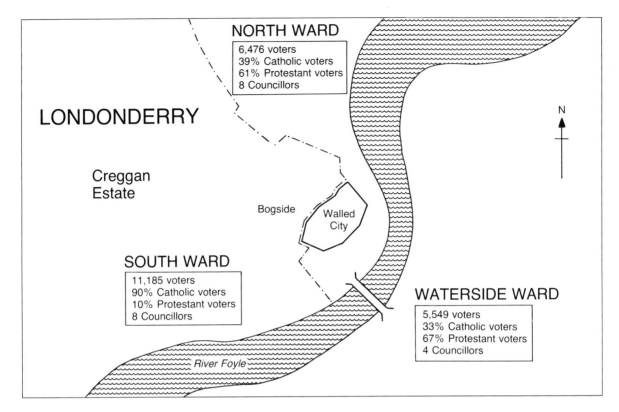

NORTH WARD
6,476 voters
39% Catholic voters
61% Protestant voters
8 Councillors

LONDONDERRY

Creggan
Estate

Bogside

Walled
City

N

SOUTH WARD
11,185 voters
90% Catholic voters
10% Protestant voters
8 Councillors

WATERSIDE WARD
5,549 voters
33% Catholic voters
67% Protestant voters
4 Councillors

River Foyle

Gerrymandering in Derry

government electoral boundaries . . . in order to achieve and maintain Unionist control of local authorities and so to deny to Catholics influence in local government proportionate to their numbers'.

As a result of these changes, the Nationalists were able to win only two councils in 1924! Even in largely Catholic areas, the Unionists won control.

Discrimination

How did the Unionists intend to use their political power? Many of them believed that if Ulster was a Protestant state, then it should be run for the good of loyal Protestants. This meant, for example, that the best jobs should be kept for Protestants, particularly when there was high unemployment in Ulster. Catholics became convinced that they were victims of **discrimination**, especially during the depression of the 1930s and the 1960s,

when Northern Ireland faced far higher unemployment than England.

SOURCE 10c

(Statements by Lord Brookeborough, Prime Minister of Ulster)

I recommend those people who are Loyalists not to employ Roman Catholics, 99 per cent of whom are disloyal. (1934)
They say why aren't we given more higher positions? But how can you give somebody who is your enemy a higher position in order to allow him to come out and destroy you? (1968)

SOURCE 10d

(Aim of Ulster Protestant Action, formed by Ian Paisley, 1959)

To keep Protestants and loyal workers in employment in times of depression in preference to their fellow Catholic workers.

SOURCE 10e

(*The Sunday Times*, 1972)

[in] Derry ... in 1966, the heads of all City Council departments were Protestant. Of 177 salaried employees, 145 – earning £124,424 – were Protestant, and only 32 – earning £20,420 – were Catholic.
... Of 10,000 workers in the Belfast shipyard – the biggest source of employment in the city – just 400 were Catholic.

By controlling government, the Unionists also had the power to build and rent council houses. Once more, Protestants tended to get the best treatment.

SOURCE 10f

(*The Sunday Times*, 1972)

There are several ways in which Protestant councils have discriminated against Catholics. One has been to put Protestants in better houses than Catholics, but charge the same rent ... Another way has simply been to house more Protestants than Catholics. Of 1,589 houses built by Fermanagh County Council between the end of the Second World War and 1969, 1,021 went to Protestant families.

The Nationalist MP, Austin Currie, highlighted this abuse in 1966 when he staged a sit-in at a new council house in Fermanagh which had just been given to the single, teenage secretary of a Unionist MP, even though there were a number of homeless Catholic families on the Council waiting list.

Discrimination against Catholics continued, even when the threat from the Republic seemed to have faded. When De Valera became **Taoiseach** (Irish Prime Minister) in 1932 he promised not to attempt to reunite Ireland by force, and soon afterwards banned the IRA. It has remained an illegal organisation in Eire ever since. Nevertheless, Unionists were concerned at the influence of the Catholic Church in the Republic, especially when the Constitution of Eire in 1937 gave it a special position. They were also outraged when Eire stayed neutral during the Second World War.

After the Second World War, though, many northern Catholics began to abandon the idea of unification. The new generation had never known a united Ireland and remembered little of the struggles of the IRA. They saw hope in the new Welfare State being created in Britain, and therefore in Ulster, with a National Health Service and increased social services. None of this was available in the poorer Republic.

SOURCE 10g

(From Eamonn McCann, *War and an Irish Town*)

Compulsory national insurance, increased family allowances and the Health Service all helped to shield Catholics from the worst effects of unemployment and poverty ... and since such benefits were not available south of the border the tendency to regard the achievement of a united Ireland as the only way to make things better began to weaken.

Support for the IRA and unification began to fade. Besides, there was little belief in the ability of Republican groups to achieve unification. The IRA was an increasingly small group of old men and the Unionists seemed more firmly entrenched than ever. So, many northern Catholics began to seek fairer treatment in Ulster rather than unification.

A bombing campaign in Britain in 1956 achieved little, and in 1959 the IRA decided to end the armed struggle.

SOURCE 10h

(The IRA calls off its campaign, 1959)

The decision to end the resistance campaign has been taken in view of the general situation. Foremost among the facts motivating this course of action has been the attitude of the general public whose minds have been deliberately distracted from the supreme issue facing the Irish people – the unity and freedom of Ireland.

SOURCE 10i

(From Patrick Bishop and Eamonn Mallie, *The Provisional IRA*, 1987)

In 1969 there were fewer than 60 men in Belfast who would regard themselves as members of the IRA . . . The low state of the movement's fortunes was illustrated by the fact that the Belfast contingent at the 1966 Wolfe Tone commemoration at Bodenstown was able to travel there by minibus.

Despite this, the Unionists were unwilling to relax their control by giving more rights to Catholics. Loyalists had never been convinced by De Valera's promises not to attempt to reunite Ireland by force, and were aware that Eire still saw a united Ireland as its eventual aim. They feared peaceful unification as much as force. Many Unionists were horrified when their Prime Minister, Terence O'Neill, met Sean Lemass, the Taoiseach of Eire in 1965. O'Neill accepted that Ulster Catholics had genuine grievances, and wanted reforms. But other leading Loyalists were very suspicious. After all, as it appeared to them, Catholics could only have more rights if loyal Protestants had less. And most Catholics were 'traitors' to Ulster.

Ian Paisley

Terence O'Neill

Was this what Carson and Craig had fought for? Ian Paisley and others began a campaign against O'Neill and against any contact with the Republic. For them, it was still a case of 'No Surrender!'

SOURCE 10j

(*New Standard*, 6 February 1981)

Ian Paisley paraded 500 men from a private Protestant army today. He said 'These men are ready to fight and die rather than accept an all-Ireland Republic. They are prepared to defend their province in the same way as Lord Carson and the men of the Ulster Volunteer Force'.

EXERCISES

1 How might a Unionist politician in the 1930s have answered each of the following questions?
   (a) Why do you think that so few Catholics are employed by Protestants?
   (b) How would you defend the system of voting in local elections in Northern Ireland?
   (c) Do you accept the view that Catholics in Northern Ireland suffer from discrimination because of their religion?
2 How does Source 10j show the importance of history to the Ulster Unionists of today?

—11—
Civil Rights

'The year 1968 was the most turbulent since the end of World War II. The entire post-war order was challenged in a chain of **insurrections** extending from America to Western Europe and Czechoslovakia.'

(David Caute, *Sixty-Eight: The Year of the Barricades*)

For Northern Ireland, 1968 was certainly a turbulent year – the first year of the phase of 'The Troubles' which continues to this day. The trouble began with Catholic demands for Civil Rights.

A Campaign for Social Justice had been founded in 1964, and in 1967 the Northern Ireland Civil Rights Association (NICRA) had been set up. But why had such groups started at this particular time? After all, the conditions about which they were protesting had existed since 1920 (see Chapter 10). And what did they mean by 'Civil Rights'?

One reason was the growth of a new generation of Catholics in Northern Ireland. These had benefited from reforms since 1944 which had increased secondary education throughout Britain. The leaders of the Civil Rights movement included many students, especially from Queen's University, Belfast.

Another reason stemmed from events far from Britain. In the southern states of America, black people had begun a campaign for Civil Rights in the late 1950s. There, Martin Luther King and his followers had used a variety of methods to attract attention to injustices. Boycotts, marches, 'sit-ins', 'freedom rides', all hit the headlines around the world. King always insisted on non-violent action, though he did believe in civil disobedience – refusing to obey unjust laws. The demonstrators often met with brutality from the white police forces, which won them further sympathy and support.

Civil Rights march, 1968

In Ulster, NICRA also claimed to be non-violent and non-sectarian, and used similar methods to show up unjust treatment of Catholics. In August 1968, the first big Civil Rights march took place when 25,000 people marched from Coalisland to Dungannon. Their demands were simple:

1 The vote for everybody as in the rest of the United Kingdom.
2 The redrawing of electoral boundaries . . . to ensure fair representation.
3 Laws against discrimination in employment at local government level.
4 A compulsory points system for housing which would ensure fair allocation.
5 The repeal of the Special Powers Act.
6 The disbanding of the B-Specials.

Protestants in Ulster were greatly concerned. Many of them felt that to give equal rights to Catholics would destroy Unionist Ulster. Many, like Ian Paisley, feared that their way of life was threatened. Many believed that the Civil Rights movement was just a 'front' for Republicans like the IRA who wanted to destroy Ulster. In 1969 Lord Cameron led a government enquiry into 'The Troubles', in which he considered these fears.

SOURCE 11a

(The Cameron Report, 1969)

It is undoubtedly the case that it has been the policy of the Northern Ireland Civil Rights Association to refuse to permit the display of provocative symbols or banners, in particular the Republican Tricolour, at any demonstration that it has organised.
    It is and always has been a basic rule of the association to place no bar on people from political groups . . . There is no doubt that the IRA has taken a close interest in the Civil Rights Association.

By the autumn of 1968, attitudes were changing. In America, Martin Luther King had been assassinated. New black groups like the Black Panthers now supported violence and there were serious riots in many American cities. All over Europe, too, student protests were becoming more and more violent, with street-fighting in Paris, Berlin and London. In Northern Ireland, groups like the Derry Housing Action Committee and People's Democracy were calling for tougher action for Civil Rights. Eamonn McCann of the Derry Housing Action Committee admitted 'our conscious, if unspoken strategy was to provoke the police into over-reaction and thus spark off mass reaction against the authorities.'
    The clash came in October 1968 when a Civil Rights march was planned in Derry. It was meant to pass through the Protestant 'Diamond' area of the city. A Protestant march was organised for the same day, and the Government banned both marches. The Civil Rights leaders decided to go ahead anyway, and the march on October 5 ended in a violent confrontation, with many people in Ireland and Britain shocked by television pictures of police beating demonstrators. The media was to have a huge impact on the interpretation of events in Northern Ireland.

SOURCE 11b

(The Nationalist MP, Bernadette Devlin, *The Price of My Soul*)

Derry was in every newspaper in Ireland, every newspaper in Britain. It was being flashed on every television screen in the world . . . And Ireland was up in arms; you can slowly crush the Irish . . . but if you hit them, they will hit back. So the Unionist Government did the civil rights movement a favour. They gave it life in one day. Without the police, it would have taken much longer to get off the ground.

SOURCE 11c

(James Callaghan, British Home Secretary in 1968)

Pictures of the extraordinary scenes of violence and fighting were flashed around the world. Ulster had arrived in the headlines.

Civil Rights march, Londonderry 5 October 1968

Violence continued. In January 1969 a Civil Rights march from Belfast to Derry was ambushed by a Protestant mob, including off-duty B-Specials, at Burntollet Bridge. Again, Catholics were left with the feeling that at best the police could not protect them; at worst, they felt that the RUC actually sided with the Loyalist mobs. The arrival of the marchers in Derry was followed by serious rioting in the Catholic Bogside area of the city – and by increased suspicion of the police.

SOURCE 11d

(Eamonn McCann on the Derry Riots, 1969)

The area was peaceful and deserted at 2am when a mob of policemen came from the city centre . . . They broke in windows with their

batons, kicked doors and shouted to the people to 'come out and fight, you Fenian bastards'. Anyone who did come to his or her door was grabbed and beaten up.

SOURCE 11e

(The Cameron Report on the Derry Riots, 1969)

Our investigations have led us to the unhesitating conclusion that on the night of 4/5 January a number of policemen were guilty of misconduct which involved assault and battery, malicious damage to property . . . and the use of provocative sectarian and political slogans.

More fighting broke out in Londonderry in the summer, as a march by the Protestant Apprentice Boys passed the Bogside on August 12. Many Catholics had little confidence in the police by now, and they started to build barricades to keep the RUC out of the area. During the 'Battle of the Bogside' Catholic youths exchanged stones and petrol bombs with police CS gas. The

The Battle of the Bogside, August 1969

The Battle of the Bogside

police failed to remove the barricades. At the same time, Catholic areas in Belfast were attacked by Protestant mobs. Over 150 homes were fire-bombed and six Catholics died.

There were two immediate results. The Unionist government had to admit that it could not control the increasing violence. It looked as though Ulster was heading for civil war. On August 14, the first British soldiers were sent to Belfast to separate the rival mobs. In the beginning they were welcomed by the Catholic community, which trusted them far more than the 'Unionist' RUC.

Secondly, when a Protestant mob attacked another Catholic area of Belfast shortly afterwards it was met not by the police, but by armed members of the Provisional IRA (see page 53). Four Loyalists were killed. When the 'Provos' (Provisionals) declared the Bogside 'Free Derry' and a 'no-go' area to the RUC, the IRA had reappeared as a major force in Northern Ireland. To many Catholics, the Provos seemed to be the only people willing and able to defend Catholic areas.

'Free Derry' – an IRA road-block

EXERCISES

1 ' . . . if the blacks of America could take on that mighty nation, we could take on a twopence-halfpenny state.' (Bernadette Devlin). Explain how this comment shows that the Civil Rights movement in Northern Ireland was inspired by black Americans.

2 For what reasons might Eamonn McCann (Source 11d) be an unreliable witness? Does Source 11e increase or decrease the reliability of McCann's version of events?

3 Write the first paragraph of two newspaper reports of the fighting in Derry on 5 October 1968. One should be for a Loyalist paper, the other for a Nationalist paper.

4 In your opinion, who was most to blame for the violence of 1968–9:
  (a) the Civil Rights movement
  (b) the Northern Ireland police force
  c) the Government of Northern Ireland?
  Explain and support your answer very carefully.

5 List all the factors that might affect the reliability of photographs and television film as historical evidence.

The Battle of the Bogside

6 Look carefully at the photographs in this chapter. Using the photographs alone as evidence, draw up a table like the one below to state whether you agree or disagree with each statement:

	Agree	Disagree	Evidence
The Civil Rights movement wanted a united Ireland			
The Civil Rights movement wanted jobs and houses			
The police used violence against demonstrators			
Children took part in the 'Battle of the Bogside'			
The IRA were unwelcome in Derry			
The police were unable to control Derry			

—12—
'The Troubles'

'Armoured cars and tanks and guns
Came to take away our sons
But every man will stand behind
The men behind the wire.'
   (Republican song against internment, 1971)

The arrival of British troops failed to end the trouble in Ulster. At first they were welcomed by most Catholics, but this was short-lived. Unionists remained in control, and the army came to be seen as just another part of the Unionist security forces, like the RUC. The hated 'B-Specials' were disbanded in 1970 and replaced by the Ulster Defence Regiment. Even so, the UDR was itself almost entirely Protestant and did little to improve Catholic confidence. In Nationalist areas the IRA was increasingly seen as the only 'army' able to defend Catholics.

The IRA was able to claim that the presence of British troops showed that Ireland was still not independent. Nationalists came to see the soldiers as an army of occupation. Army tactics in dealing with rioting, especially the use of CS gas and rubber bullets, increased support for the IRA. In February 1971 the first British soldier since the arrival of the army was killed by the IRA.

'The Troubles' caused O'Neill to resign and in August 1971 a new Stormont government led by Brian Faulkner decided on a new policy – internment. On 9 August, 342 men suspected of involvement in 'The Troubles' were arrested and taken to the 'H-Blocks' of Long Kesh camp. Internment meant that suspects could be held in prison for any length of time without a trial. Of the 342 arrested, 226 were interned. Only two were Protestants. Catholics again felt that they were being treated unfairly.

By December, 1,576 people had been interned. This had been accompanied by a wave of violence, and by protests about the system in Ireland and Britain. Was it fair to deny suspects a trial? Many internees also complained of ill-treatment. A British Government inquiry concluded that prisoners had indeed suffered 'physical ill-treatment', but rejected charges of 'brutality' against the security forces. In January 1978 the European Court of Human Rights found that there had been no torture of internees, but that Britain was guilty of 'inhuman and degrading' treatment of prisoners.

'Bloody Sunday'

On Sunday, January 30 1972, a large crowd of Civil Rights marchers gathered in Derry to protest against internment. The Unionist government had banned all marches in August, and the army was sent to prevent the march from reaching the Guildhall from the Bogside. Fighting began as the marchers were met by barricades manned by men from the Parachute Regiment. By the end of the day, 13 civilians had been killed by army bullets.

The events of 'Bloody Sunday' outraged the Nationalist community. It was followed by more rioting and recruitment for the IRA, which now saw British soldiers as 'legitimate targets'. In the House of Commons, the Home Secretary was attacked by the Nationalist MP, Bernadette Devlin; in Dublin, an angry crowd burned down the British Embassy. 'Bloody Sunday' soon joined the long list of dates in Ireland's history to be remembered with

'Bloody Sunday'

bitterness and anger.

It also helped to make the problem of Ulster a British problem again. In March 1972, the Northern Ireland Government was dissolved, and direct rule from Britain was introduced. Just as in the years 1880–1920, Northern Irish MPs were to attend Westminster.

Internment and the actions of the security forces also served to revive Republicanism among Ulster Catholics. This in turn revived the fortunes of the IRA, who once again turned to 'the armed struggle' against the British.

SOURCE 12a

(A volunteer explains why he joined the IRA. From an interview in *The Guardian*, 14 August 1989)

I was about eight when it all began. I remember the British Army coming in and I remember being harrassed. I felt I wanted to do something . . . I would never have been involved in violence had it not been for the British presence. I don't feel our country should be governed by a foreign country. The means was the IRA and I volunteered.

'The Troubles' continued. A series of explosions took place in Belfast and Derry. On one day alone, 21 July 1972, 'Bloody Friday', about 300 people were injured when 22 bombs went off in 45 minutes around Belfast city centre. The Provisionals 'succeeded in reducing the centre of Derry to rubble'. Near the border, in South

An IRA sniper

An army patrol in Derry

Armagh, Provisional attacks caused the area to be known as 'bandit country'. The army gave up attempting to move around by road – helicopters became their only safe method of transport. As well as attacking their enemies in Ulster, the IRA also decided to try to change public opinion in Britain by 'bringing the war to England' with a series of bombings in England itself.

In the 20 years since the start of the current 'Troubles' there have been more and more 'anniversaries' to add to the divisions in Northern Ireland. Between 1989 and the arrival of British troops in Derry in August 1969, 2,761 people in Northern Ireland met violent deaths. By 1989 there were 10,800 British troops stationed in Northern Ireland, along with 6,400 soldiers of the UDR.

Views of 'Bloody Sunday'

SOURCE 12b

(Lt.-Col. Wilford, Commander of No. 1 Para on 'Bloody Sunday')

It's unfortunate but when we got up there past William Street, here . . . and up towards Rossville

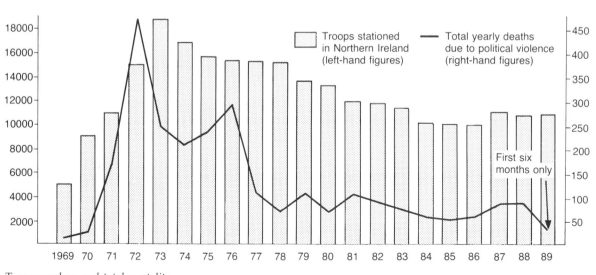

Troop numbers and total mortality

Flats we came under fire . . . we were also petrol bombed, and some acid, in fact, was poured on us from the top of the Flats. When we're fired at, we must protect ourselves.

SOURCE 12c

(Father Bradley, a Catholic priest)

It was a massacre. I saw no shooting at troops. If anybody had been, I would have seen it. I saw only the Army shooting. The British Army should hang its head in shame after today's disgusting violence. They shot **indiscriminately** and everywhere around them without any provocation.

SOURCE 12d

(Simon Winchester, writing about 'Bloody Sunday' in *The Guardian*)

I do not think, from what I saw, that the IRA opened up first, other than one shot which was fired in William Street. Even if they did, I do not think it would have justified the return of fire into crowds of people in that packed square. I saw three people hit, but I honestly and truly could not see any guns. Nor did I hear any nail bombs or petrol bombs being thrown. I have heard many of these and I know the noise they make.

SOURCE 12e

(Nigel Wade, writing about 'Bloody Sunday' in *The Daily Telegraph*)

I was one of more than 1,000 people lying flat on their faces as the shooting continued. Pinned to the ground, it was impossible to tell who fired the first shots . . .

SOURCE 12f

(Lord Widgery, a British judge who investigated 'Bloody Sunday' for the British Government)

Each soldier was his own judge of whether he had identified a gunman . . . At one end of the scale, some soldiers showed a high degree of responsibility, at the other . . . firing bordered on the reckless.

SOURCE 12g

(Londonderry City Coroner at inquest)

It strikes me that the army ran amok that day . . . They were shooting innocent people. These people may have been taking part in a parade that was banned – but I don't think that justifies the firing of live rounds indiscriminately. I say it without reservation – it was sheer unadulterated [pure] murder.

SOURCE 12h

(From Patrick Bishop and Eamonn Mallie, *The Provisional IRA*, 1987)

Soldiers who were there still maintain that they heard the sound of . . . fire before the Paras opened up. The men leading the Derry IRA at the time are equally insistent that no IRA action took place that day. Almost the entire membership of the Derry units . . . was on the march and the likelihood of being arrested or searched meant that none of them were armed . . . None of the men hit was wanted by the security forces.

EXERCISES

1 (a) What are the important differences in the views of 'Bloody Sunday' given in Source 12b and Source 12c? What reasons can you suggest for these differences? If witnesses disagree does it mean that somebody must be lying?
(b) How many of the sources above appear to be biased? Explain how you can tell. Will a biased witness always be unreliable?

2 How does the evidence of the reporters in Sources 12d and 12e differ from Sources 12b and 12c? How would you explain this?

3 (a) Why are there so many different conclusions about the same event?
(b) From the evidence provided, can you be certain about what happened on 'Bloody Sunday'?
(c) What further evidence might help you to discover what really happened on 'Bloody Sunday'?

—13—
Nationalist and Loyalist

In many ways, the problem in Northern Ireland today remains as it was in the days of Gladstone and Parnell. Just as Gladstone faced the Fenians, so todays' politicians face the violence of the IRA and UVF. The two sides are still divided by religion, economics and politics.

The Republic of Ireland is a mainly Catholic state; Northern Ireland has a Protestant majority which fears and distrusts Catholicism. Most Protestants think that the Catholic Church in Eire has too much power, especially in education and 'moral issues' like divorce and family planning. Others simply believe Catholicism is 'wrong'.

SOURCE 13a

(A Paisleyite view: Mrs. Hamilton, *Only the Rivers Run Free* 1984)

You see the Roman Catholic Church is the anti-Christ. There isn't really a political solution, because it's a religious battle against the rising of the anti-Christ.

SOURCE 13b

(From a speech by Noel Browne, Irish Labour Party, 1971)

We must recognise the genuine fears of the Northern Protestant that in a united Ireland he would be in a minority and that he would suffer in much the same way as the Catholic minority in Ulster. There is the position of the Catholic Church. There are the Catholic rules on mixed marriages, the right to contraception and family planning, the right to divorce.

Economic questions remain. Ulster has a high unemployment rate, and many Loyalists still share the views of Lord Brookeborough and Ulster Protestant Action (see page 40). Recent Government

Ian Paisley leading a Protestant march, 1960

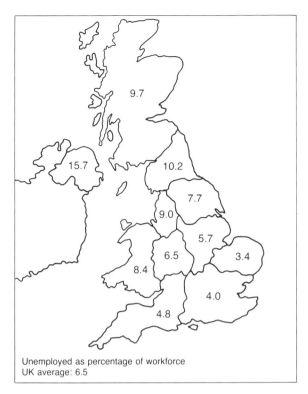

Unemployed as percentage of workforce
UK average: 6.5

Unemployment in the UK, April 1989

statistics showed that 36 per cent of male Catholics were unemployed, compared to 14 per cent of male Protestants. Attempts by the Government to end discrimination against Catholics have been strongly resisted by Protestant workers and Loyalist politicians. In housing, too, a study carried out in 1989 showed Protestants in the Belfast area to be almost twice as likely as Catholics to be rehoused.

Finally, of course, the two communities have very different ideas about who should rule Ulster. Unionists are as determined to remain part of Britain as they were in the days of Carson. Republicans still insist that Ulster can only be seen as part of a united Irish Republic.

As we saw at the start of this book, when most of you think of Northern Ireland today, or read about it in the newspapers, you almost certainly think of violence. You have almost certainly heard of the IRA. You might have heard of the UVF or INLA. So who are these groups, and what are their aims?

The best known group in Britain is the Irish Republican Army. Although the 'Official' IRA gave up the armed struggle in 1959 (except briefly in 1972, after 'Bloody Sunday'), 'The Troubles' saw a split. A new group, the 'Provisional' IRA, returned to physical force. Their aim is the traditional Republican one of reuniting Ireland and getting the British out. But their methods have been a mixture of the traditional tactics of the old IRA and of modern terrorism. The 'Provos' have tried to make it impossible for the British to govern Northern Ireland. Attacks on the army, the police, judges, members of the UDR and so on are very similar to those of the IRA between 1919 and 1922.

The other major Republican **paramilitary** group is the Irish National Liberation Army (INLA), which broke away from the Official IRA in 1975. In 1989, another Republican group appeared – the Irish People's Liberation Organisation (IPLO).

While these organisations are illegal, the IRA is spoken for by Sinn Fein, a legal political party in Northern Ireland. Since the Hunger Strikes of 1981 (see page 57) Sinn Fein has done well in local elections, taking about 40 per cent of the Nationalist vote in 1983 and winning control of a number of councils. Gerry Adams, the President of Sinn Fein, was elected as an MP, though, like Sinn Fein MPs in 1918, he has refused to take his seat in Parliament. Danny Morrison of Sinn Fein has commented on its connection with IRA violence: 'Is there anyone here who objects to taking power with a ballot paper in one hand an an Armalite rifle in the other?'

But although the IRA is the group best known in Britain, most of the bombings and killings have taken place in Northern Ireland itself. Nor has it been only Nationalist groups who have carried them out. Since 'The Troubles' began in 1969, Loyalists have killed roughly twice as many civilians as Republicans have.

Even before the appearance of the Provisional IRA, the Loyalist Ulster Volunteer Force had been reformed in 1966, with the threat that 'known IRA men will be executed mercilessly and without hesitation'. In June 1966 UVF gunmen shot three Catholics – killing one – whom they wrongly believed to be IRA leaders. The UVF was made an illegal organisation in 1975.

The Ulster Defence Association was formed in 1971, in reply to the Provisional IRA, and carried out a series of attacks on Catholics before 1979. Like Sinn Fein, the UDA is a legal organisation. Like Sinn Fein, it too has a military wing – the Ulster Freedom Fighters.

Ulster Vanguard was set up in 1972, with the aim of 'exterminating' the IRA. Another Loyalist group is Protestant Action. All of them, Nationalist or Loyalist, use very much the same methods – bombings and shootings. The aim of the Nationalists is to force the British out, while the Loyalists aim to keep Ulster British and to oppose the Republicans.

There have been many 'tit-for-tat' sectarian killings – revenge attacks for other incidents. Often the victims are chosen at random, simply because they belong to 'the other side'. In 1972 alone, 82 Catholics and 40 Protestants died in sectarian attacks. 1988 and 1989 have seen another upsurge in sectarian violence.

SOURCE 13c

(From Tim Pat Coogan, *The IRA*, 1971)

The more havoc the IRA wreaked, the more the Loyalists lashed out at Catholics – any Catholics – and the more action and reaction intertwined, the more callous everyone got.

The activities of these organisations have divided Northern Ireland more than ever. Mixed housing estates in Derry and Belfast have largely disappeared, as both Catholic and Protestant families have been forced into their own **ghettos** for fear of attacks by the paramilitary groups. Protestants and

Catholics attend separate schools, use different pubs and shops, and generally have little contact with each other.

SOURCE 13d

(*The Guardian*, 14 August 1989)

'But you can't go out with a Catholic,' one girl explained on reflection, 'because they'll have the holy water on you and you'll be in the IRA . . .'. Another said her parents would kill her if she married a Catholic. Another said he'd rear his kids not to go out with 'Fenian bastards'. One or two thought they could tell a Catholic a mile off.

By no means everybody in Northern Ireland supports the paramilitaries. The majority of Catholics have voted since 1970 for the Social Democratic and Labour Party, a Nationalist party seeking peaceful change, not for Sinn Fein. Most Protestants are supporters of one of the Unionist parties, but are not connected with groups like the UVF. There was also much support for the Peace People, formed by Betty Williams and Mairead Corrigan in 1976. They were awarded the Nobel Peace Prize for their efforts in 1977 – but they were denounced both by the IRA and the Paisleyites.

EXERCISES

1 Explain what you understand by 'sectarian violence'. Why are ordinary Catholics and Protestants in Northern Ireland likely to be attacked?
2 'The English people just don't see it as a problem except when a British soldier is killed'.
(a) Look carefully at newspaper and television reports about Northern Ireland. Do they mention Republican terrorists more often than Loyalist terrorists?
(b) Explain what you understand by the quotation above. Do you agree?

—14—
Terrorism

(Top) Yasser Arafat, Robert Mugabe, Eamonn De Valera; (bottom) Yitzhak Shamir, Nelson Mandela

To many people in Britain the problem of Northern Ireland can seem to be the problem of dealing with 'terrorism'. But what is a terrorist?

How many of these people are terrorists? At some time or other all of them have been called terrorists. Several have gone on to become leaders of their countries. How can this be explained?

Oliver Cromwell certainly used terror to subdue the Irish rebellion of the 1640s. Was he a terrorist? The Black and Tans created terror in large parts of Ireland around 1920. Were they terrorists? Were the Fenians terrorists? Were members of the French Resistance who bombed cafés used by German soldiers during the Second World War terrorists?

According to the British Government in 1974, terrorism was 'the use of violence for political ends'. According to Mrs Thatcher in 1981 'there is no such thing as political murder, political bombing or political violence'.

1971	UVF kills 15 Catholics in bombing at McGurk's bar.
	First British soldier killed by IRA.
1972	Official IRA kills 7 at Aldershot barracks.
1974	Provisional IRA kills 26 in Birmingham and Guildford pub bombings.
1975	UVF made an illegal organisation.
1979	Conservative MP Airey Neave killed by INLA.
	Lord Mountbatten killed by IRA.
	18 soldiers killed by IRA at Warrenpoint.
1982	8 soldiers killed in Hyde Park and Regent's Park bombings.
1983	5 killed in IRA bomb attack at Harrods.
1984	IRA bombs the Conservative Party conference in Brighton. 5 killed.
1985	'Miami Showband' pop group ambushed and killed by UVF.
1987	11 killed by IRA bomb at Enniskillen Remembrance Day ceremony.
1988	14 soldiers killed in two bomb attacks.
1989	2 leading RUC officers killed by IRA.
1990	IRA campaign against British targets in Europe.

Is there any difference between a member of the IRA and someone who shoots a policeman during a bank robbery?

Would 'terrorists' use the word to describe themselves?

SOURCE 14a

(Martin McGuiness, Sinn Fein, 1985)

We believe the only way the Irish people can bring about the freedom of their country is through the use of arms . . . It will be the cutting edge of the IRA that will bring freedom.

SOURCE 14b

(Patrick Bishop and Eamonn Mallie, *The Provisional IRA*, 1987)

The IRA's members sincerely believe themselves to be soldiers . . . It is as unrewarding to expect remorse from a 'volunteer' over the killing of a policeman or a politician as it is to expect regret from a soldier who shoots a sniper or a minister who allows a hunger striker to die.

SOURCE 14c

(From an interview in *The Guardian*, 14 August 1989)

I'm in the UFF, the military wing of the UDA. I am a freedom fighter, not a terrorist or a guerrilla.

Clerkenwell, 1867: The Fenians

— 56 —

Both Republican and Loyalist groups have a military organisation. Both talk of members 'on active service'. Both agree that captured members should be treated as political prisoners, not 'ordinary prisoners'. At present, three-quarters of all prisoners in Northern Ireland are serving sentences for offences linked to paramilitary activity. Between 1974 and 1976, convicted 'terrorists' were treated as 'Special Category' prisoners with certain privileges, such as being allowed to wear their own clothing and not having to do prison work. The loss of this status led to the 'Blanket Protest' by IRA prisoners who refused to wear prison uniform and wrapped themselves in blankets instead. They were joined by some Loyalist paramilitaries.

This led to the IRA Hunger Strike of 1981, the revival of an old tactic used in the 1920s. The first IRA hunger striker, Bobby Sands, was elected MP for Fermanagh with a large majority in April 1981. Did the voters believe he was a terrorist? His death on 5 May, quickly followed by nine others, led to riots in Northern Ireland and world-wide publicity. Over 50,000 people attended his funeral.

The murder of Airey Neave, 1979: INLA

Support for the IRA 'Blanketmen'

Funeral of hunger striker Tom McElwee, 1981

SOURCE 14d

(Danny Morrison, Sinn Fein, March 1981)

He [Sands] knows that if he dies, through his death, there will be so much anger stored up in the Irish people that it will fuel the struggle for the next ten years.

SOURCE 14e

(Daithi O'Connaill, Sinn Fein, December 1981)

The H-Block issue became a worldwide issue. The Republican movement gained enormously in the number of people who joined, in favourable publicity and in finance.

SOURCE 14f

(*Die Arbeiter Zeitung*, Austria)

They were considered terrorists, now they are martyrs.

SOURCE 14g

(*Ta Nea*, Greece)

You cannot help admiring a man who has the guts to die this way for a political aim.

The trial of Michael Stone, 1989. Loyalists chant their support outside the court.

It seems that the gunmen of both sides have support from their communities. 'Terrorist' prisoners are viewed as heroes and martyrs. Most Republicans are familiar with the names of the ten dead hunger strikers. Huge crowds attend the funerals of dead volunteers like Tom McElwee or the three members of the IRA killed by the SAS under suspicion of organising a bombing attack in Gibraltar. Michael Stone has become a Loyalist hero, glorified in paintings and a ballad in Loyalist areas of Belfast.

MICHAEL Stone, the "freelance" Loyalist gunman who wanted to murder the IRA leadership at Milltown Cemetery in March last year, was yesterday given six concurrent life sentences with a recommendation that he serve at least 30 years.

Stone, aged 33, launched a gun and grenade attack on mourners at the funerals of the three IRA terrorists shot by the SAS in Gibraltar. Three Catholics were killed and a further 68 people were injured. He also murdered three other Catholics between 1984 and last year.

Stone, of Ravenswood Park, east Belfast, stood impassively as Mr Justice Eoin Higgins pronounced judgement at Belfast Crown Court. He had refused to allow his counsel, Mr Desmond Boal, QC, to speak on his behalf.

The judge had hardly finished when he gave a clenched fist salute, shouting "Long live Ulster. No surrender."

Loyalist supporters in the public gallery cheered while a small group of relatives of those killed at Milltown clapped and shouted "Tiocfaidh ar La", Gaelic for "Our Day will come".

The trial of Michael Stone, 1989

SOURCE 14h

(From Bishop and Mallie, *The Provisional IRA*)

Even if the leadership [of the Provisional IRA] were to abandon violence, another violent Republican organisation would spring up in its place. As long as Ireland is divided, violent Republicanism will be an ineradicable tradition [one which cannot be wiped out].

And so, of course, will militant Unionism.

A number of prominent Loyalists (including the man on the right in this photograph) were arrested in Paris and charged with trying to buy weapons from South Africa.

EXERCISES

1 Look carefully at the photograph of Tom McElwee's funeral and the extract about the trial of Michael Stone. Now look at the list of words below. Pick out the words that you think the supporters of McElwee and Stone would use to describe them. Then pick out the words that you think their opponents would use. Explain your choices carefully.

Terrorist   Hero   Guerrilla
Murderer   Freedom fighter   Criminal

2 Outline the arguments for and against treating captured 'terrorists' as political prisoners.

3 Source 14h calls violent Republicanism 'an ineradicable tradition'. What other examples of this tradition can you remember from earlier chapters? How do the Provisional IRA fit into this tradition?

—15—
Any Answers?

When the first British soldiers were sent into Londonderry in 1969, they did not expect to be there 20 years later. So far, Ireland has remained impossible to 'pacify'. Are there any answers to the Irish Question?

Is it simply a question of 'law-and-order'? There have been a number of changes made to the law in Northern Ireland in an attempt to deal with the problems caused by 'The Troubles'. Since 1973, trials in terrorist cases have not been decided by jury. Guilt or innocence is decided by a single judge under the 'Diplock rules'. Members of the jury could be threatened too easily by the paramilitaries. In another attempt to make it easier to get evidence the police began to use 'Supergrasses' – informers from within the IRA or UVF. This, however, was abandoned after a number of these witnesses were shown to be unreliable.

There has also been an effort to make it easier to **extradite** suspects from other countries to face trial in Britain. This has met problems, though, as the extract opposite indicates.

Suspicions about the evidence used in some cases have also been raised. Four people imprisoned after the Guildford pub bombings of 1974 had their convictions quashed and were freed in 1989, and many people believe that the 'Birmingham Six' were wrongly convicted of similar offences, also in 1974.

In addition, the police have extra powers under the Prevention of Terrorism Act of 1974. This allows them to hold suspects without charge for longer than the normal period in Britain. Certain individuals can also be banned from entering Northern Ireland or travelling from Ulster to mainland Britain. Like so much since 1969 this was meant to be a temporary measure,

GOVERNMENT lawyers have concluded that Father Patrick Ryan's chances of a fair trial on terrorist charges in Britain last year were seriously prejudiced by Mrs Thatcher.

They believe that the Prime Minister's intervention contributed to the decision by Mr John Murray, the Irish Attorney-General, to refuse to give up Father Ryan, wanted on charges of murder and causing explosions.

The Prime Minister's comments, combined with those of Conservative MPs and reports in the British media, according to British government lawyers, would have allowed Father Ryan to claim successfully that he would not have got a fair trial in Britain.

Problems with extradition: The Guardian, *14 April 1989*

but has now become permanent.

Is a military solution possible? Gladstone found that 'the resources of civilisation' could not end unrest. Lloyd George was advised by his generals that a military victory over the IRA was impossible. Most army officers today also believe that only a political solution can end the violence. Some of the methods used by the Security Forces have led to fierce debate. Nationalists have been angered by suspicions of a 'shoot-to-kill' policy (as opposed to shooting in self-defence or with intent to wound only), as when six unarmed 'volunteers' were killed in 1981. More recently, the killing of three unarmed IRA members by the SAS in Gibraltar caused great controversy. Does this bring back memories of the Black and Tans?

There has been concern, too, over the use of rubber and plastic bullets in riot control. These weapons have killed 17 people since

Gibraltar inquest verdict criticised by Amnesty

IRA bombers 'failed to understand garbled shout'

SAS men fired after 'useless' warning

SAS accused of lying to police over IRA killings

Soldier denies shooting at Savage after he fell

The Gibraltar affair, 1988

The Hillsborough Agreement

1969, including a number of children, and injured many more.

Or could the answer be for the British to withdraw the army from Northern Ireland? For Republicans, of course, this is the first step towards a solution. Many people in Britain, too, would favour this. Most Loyalists, however, are fiercely opposed to the idea of withdrawal.

Is there a political solution? When Direct Rule was introduced to Northern Ireland in 1972 it was meant to be a temporary answer to an emergency. It was linked with a number of reforms, including disbanding the B-Specials and the end of gerrymandering, and with tough measures like internment.

With this background, Edward Heath's government suggested a system of 'power sharing' in 1973. This would have given Catholics some say in the government of Northern Ireland. The 'Sunningdale Agreement', however, was strongly opposed by the hard-line Unionists of the Democratic Unionist Party and the Ulster Workers' Council. A Loyalist general strike early in 1974 led to the collapse of the new system. This, in fact, also suited the Republicans, for whom power sharing was no solution at all: nothing less than the unification of Ireland would be acceptable to the IRA and Sinn Fein.

A second attempt at a political solution began in 1985, when the British Government signed the 'Anglo-Irish

WHAT SHOULD NORTHERN IRELAND'S FUTURE BE?

REMAIN PART OF UK	BECOME INDEPENDENT	UNION WITH REPUBLIC	DON'T KNOW
29%	29%	27%	15%

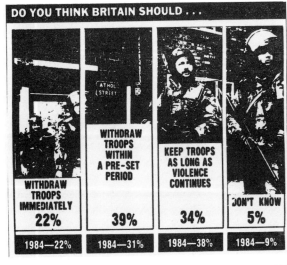

DO YOU THINK BRITAIN SHOULD . . .

WITHDRAW TROOPS IMMEDIATELY	WITHDRAW TROOPS WITHIN A PRE-SET PERIOD	KEEP TROOPS AS LONG AS VIOLENCE CONTINUES	DON'T KNOW
22%	39%	34%	5%
1984—22%	1984—31%	1984—38%	1984—9%

Troops Out? MORI poll, Daily Express, *10 February 1987*

Agreement' (Hillsborough Agreement) with Eire. This aimed at more co-operation between Britain and Eire over matters like policing and security in the border areas. Once more, both Republicans and hard-line Loyalists objected. The Loyalists feared any involvement in the affairs of Ulster by Dublin, just as they had protested so strongly about the visit of Sean Lemass in 1965, and feared 'betrayal' by Britain. The Republicans equally feared 'betrayal' by the South, echoing their divisions in 1920.

SOURCE 15a

(*The Guardian*, 21 November 1985)

The Northern Ireland Secretary, Mr Tom King, was attacked and abused yesterday outside and inside Belfast City Hall in a series of incidents which Loyalist demonstrators promised was a taste of things to come ... some elected politicians from the Official and Democratic Unionist parties had to be physically restrained by police from getting at the Secretary of State. Others satisfied themselves with shouts of 'traitor' and a continual chant of 'Dublin out' ... the Reverend Ian Paisley, who had quickly appeared at the scene of the trouble, warned: 'I do not believe it is prudent or sane for Mr King to be seen anywhere in Northern Ireland. The more he is seen, the more he is inciting the people of Northern Ireland.'

SOURCE 15b

(Ian Paisley fears 'betrayal' 24 November 1985)

The hearts of Ulster have been stricken with the deepest of sorrows. Mrs Thatcher tells us that the Republic has got a say in this province. We say never, never, never, never. We are prepared to lay down our lives for Ulster. I never thought I would live to see the day when 1912 was repeated.

SOURCE 15c

(Gerry Adams, President of Sinn Fein, rejects the Hillsborough Agreement, 16 November 1985)

This deal does not go anywhere near bringing peace to this part of Ireland. On the contrary it reinforces partition because Dublin is recognising Northern Ireland.

What about the part to be played in the future by education? Can the schools help to break down centuries of sectarianism? Recently a number of new integrated schools, taking both Catholic and Protestant pupils, have been opened in Northern Ireland. Will they eventually help the two communities to understand each other better?

Could a united Ireland ever work in the face of such a history of bitterness, division and sectarianism? On the other hand, can Northern Ireland continue for ever in its present form, facing more violence and major economic problems? Or might it be possible to create an independent Ulster, part of neither Britain nor Eire?

EXERCISES

1 Here are four possible solutions to the question of Northern Ireland.
   (a) Return to the situation between 1920–72: Northern Ireland remains part of the UK but with its own government.
   (b) Make Northern Ireland a full part of the UK, with no special institutions (like Wales and Scotland).
   (c) Unite Northern Ireland with the Republic of Ireland.
   (d) Make Northern Ireland an independent state, with no connection with either the UK or the Republic of Ireland.
   For each of these, make a list of the advantages and disadvantages. Which of these solutions would you suggest, and why?
2 'We're all prisoners of history here'. Write a short essay to explain the ways in which history still affects the attitudes and ideas of both Nationalists and Loyalists in Northern Ireland today. Mention the main historical events which will be important to each group, what they will mean to them and why they continue to be so important.

Glossary

ascendancy   domination

barbarous   cruel, primitive

boycott   refusing to have anything to do with someone

coalition   a government made up of two or more parties

commemorate   remember with public honour

denominational   belonging to one religious group

discrimination   treating a person or group differently – often unfairly

dissident   someone who objects to a government

dupes   fools

emancipation   freedom

encroach   move gradually forward

extortion   obtaining something through threats or violence

extradite   return a suspect from one country for trial in another

Gaelic   descended from the Celts

ghetto   a district lived in by people belonging to one group

guerrilla   member of a small, independent fighting group

imperialism   when one country rules another

indiscriminately   carelessly

insurrection   rebellion

internment   imprisonment without trial

manifesto   declaration of policy

martyr   someone who suffers or dies for a belief

pacify   calm down, bring about peace

papists   a Protestant term for Roman Catholics

paramilitary   a member of an organisation using political violence

proportional representation   a voting system based on the percentage of votes for each party (eg, a party with 30% of the votes has 30% of the seats)

sectarian   divided into religious or political groups

shamrock   small three-leafed plant – a national symbol of Ireland

stereotype   assuming all members of a group to be alike

subjection   rule by force

Taoiseach   title of Prime Minister of Eire

tyrant   a cruel ruler

Index